BLESSED AND UNSTOPPABLE

YOUR BLUEPRINT FOR SUCCESS

*Dream Big!
With God, All Things Are Possible!
May God Bless You Always,
Billy Alsbrooks
Jeremiah 29:11*

BLESSED AND UNSTOPPABLE

YOUR BLUEPRINT FOR SUCCESS

#BillyAlsbrooks

144 Crawl Key Court • Deland, FL 32720
www.billyalsbrooks.com

Scripture taken from THE HOLY BIBLE, NEW INTERNATIONAL VERSION®. Copyright © 1973, 1978, 1984 by International Bible Society. Used by permission of International Bible Society. All rights reserved.

"NIV" and "NEW INTERNATIONAL VERSION" are trademarks registered in the United States Patent and Trademark office by International Bible Society.

Scripture taken from The Holy Bible, English Standard Version (ESV). Copyright © 2001 by Crossway, a publishing ministry of Good News Publishers. All rights reserved.

Scripture taken from the King James Version.

Scripture taken from New Life Version (NLV) Copyright © Christian Literature International. All rights reserved.

Blessed and Unstoppable: Your Blueprint for Success

Published by:

144 Crawl Key Court
Deland, FL 32720
(407)310-3275

2017© Billy Alsbrooks
Printed in U.S.A.
ISBN: 978-0-9982874-4-7

All rights reserved. No part of this book may be reproduced by any means, nor transmitted, nor translated into a machine language without the express written permission of the Publisher or Author.

Success is a marathon of consistency, walked out one day at a time.

#BillyAlsbrooks

Who We Are:
Positive Worldwide is a Christian based company that specializes in inspiring products that educate, motivate, and empower people to become all that God designed them to be.

Our Vision:
Positive Worldwide will become the most effective success engineering company in the world. We will equip people with the tools needed to become successful, and then motivate them to do the actions required to achieve it.

Our Mission:
Educate • Motivate • Empower

Our Slogan:
Impact Lives Daily!

Our Core Values:
Wisdom • Faith • Integrity • Passion
Motivation • Education • Excellence

Our Long Term Aspirations:
We will build the online self-help capital of the world by consistently delivering the most effective content for personal transformation. As our company grows, we will add more value by expanding into other areas such as books, radio, TV, video, live streaming, clothing, mobile apps, etc. We will launch our Blessed Buddies brand to do for kids what we do for adults. Through many different platforms Blessed Buddies will connect with children teaching them in fun, positive, and entertaining ways the principles for success.

TABLE OF CONTENTS:

Introduction..9
To Get the Most Out of this Book........................10
The Success Teachings...13
The Self-Awareness Workbook..........................177
Bringing Your Life into Focus.............................193
Wisdom for Achieving Greatness......................203
The Power to Overcome......................................225
Aligning with the Blessing..................................257
How to Walk in Victory.......................................299

B7UCLOTHING.COM

INTRODUCTION:

This book has been strategically designed to align your mind with the laws of success. Consistently applying these principles will create the environment needed for you to prosper and thrive. By accepting and adhering to the truth written on these pages, every area of your existence will be impacted. As you follow this guide step by step, amazing breakthroughs will happen, new doors of opportunity will open, and favor will begin to chase you down.

Blessed and Unstoppable will instigate the thought process and actions required to transform your life. It's packed full of time tested prosperity wisdom presented in a way that you can easily understand. The purpose of this material is to educate, motivate, and empower you with the tools and strategies needed to accomplish your dreams. This curriculum will teach you the inner mechanics required to go from average to phenomenal, from living a life with limits to being blessed and unstoppable. Regardless of what field you're in, this is your blueprint for success!

This massive *action* course is effectively divided into seven learning sections.

The Success Teachings: This is a 31 day devotional on the laws of success. Each day has a bible verse, a teaching on that day's principle, a positive affirmation, a prayer for the day, self-assessment questions, success quotes, actions steps, and an inspirational message.

Self-Awareness Workbook: Packed full of thought-provoking questions, this workbook will help you identify your strengths, find your passion, and better understand who you really are.

Bringing Your Life Into Focus: The material in this section will help you create a powerful vision for your life, develop your mission statement, and clarify your goals.

Wisdom for Achieving Greatness: This section contains profound insight from the author on how to become all that God created you to be.

The Power to Overcome: Separated by topics, this reference tool makes it easy to find the appropriate bible verses needed to overcome any situation.

Aligning With The Blessing: This topical bible will enable you to quickly reference what God's word says to do in every area of your life.

How to Walk in Victory: The final section includes a list of The Ten Commandments, a summary of God's law, lays out the nine fruits of the spirit, explains the three steps to receiving salvation, and ends with the sinner's prayer.

To Get The Most Out Of This Book:

The questions you ask yourself will determine the level of success you experience. To capture the full benefits of this program, set time aside to think, meditate, and ponder on the powerful self-assessment part of this book. These questions will set your mind in motion, creating the mental energy needed to shift your mindset. The same paradigms and belief systems that create loss, lack, and failure will not produce success. Success can only be attained with thoughts and actions that consistently correlate with it. Half the battle of achieving prosperity is finding the right questions to ask yourself. This program does that for you, all you have to do is the inner homework required to discover your own answers. If you are really serious about changing your life, commit yourself fully to working on and applying the steps in this book!

31 Steps to Success

1. Detox Emotionally
2. Get Alone with God Daily
3. Adopt the Mindset of the Unstoppable
4. Define Your Core Values
5. Create a Powerful Vision
6. Follow Your Passion
7. Awaken to Your Calling
8. Speak the Language of Heaven
9. Find Your Why
10. Raise Your Standard
11. Master Yourself
12. Plug into the Power
13. Stay in Your Lane
14. Go All In
15. Assemble Wise Counsel
16. Unify Your Focus
17. Set Massive Goals
18. Destroy the Enemy Within
19. Leverage Every Second of Time
20. Declare the Blessing
21. Let Your Grind do all the Talking
22. Chase Wisdom
23. Conquer the Now
24. Exercise Your Authority
25. Build a Strong Inner Circle
26. Refuse to Concede
27. Take the Limits off God
28. Learn the Art of Communication
29. Align with Gratitude
30. Become a Prayer Warrior
31. Impact Lives Daily

BLESSED AND UNSTOPPABLE

THE SUCCESS TEACHINGS

— Day One —
DETOX EMOTIONALY

Bible Verse:
Get rid of all bitterness, rage and anger, brawling and slander, along with every form of malice. Be kind and compassionate to one another, forgiving each other, just as in Christ God forgave you.
Ephesians 4:31-32

Unforgiveness is volunteered emotional incarceration. It's a spiritual self-imprisonment behind invisible bars for which you determine your own release date. This emotional baggage is an internal ticking time bomb capable of totally destroying you. All evidence of it must be confronted and completely eradicated. Bitterness and guilt are deadly self-destructive poisons that destabilize and enslave you. You will not be able to tote those extra carry-on bags from the past into the Promised Land. They do not serve you and are not allowed on the success journey.

Forgiveness is dialysis for the soul. It's medicine from heaven. Mastering the art of letting go will create a peace inside you that surpasses all understanding. Refuse to give the devil a foothold in your life. Whether it's the burden of self-guilt or deep feelings of resentment towards someone else, forgiveness is the only way to bring your mind and body back into alignment. Detoxing emotionally releases a supernatural healing that frees you from all chains of limitation. Letting go is a choice that supernaturally empowers you to prosper and thrive.

Understand that denial is not the same thing as forgiveness. To deny is to suppress, to forgive is to acknowledge the transgression, but to overcome it with love. Letting go is undeniable evidence that you value your mental and emotional wellbeing more than the traumatic mistreatment you endured in the past. Forgiveness doesn't mean you agree with the wrong done to you, it just declares that you refuse to be held in bondage by it any longer.

Peace is the best gift you can ever give yourself. By releasing all the undealt with negative energy from the past you are sending out a clear definite message to the universe that says "I am now ready for success." Refuse to let your future be held hostage by petty personal dilemmas. Leave the past in the past where it belongs. This is not about the perpetrator who hurt you, this is about liberating yourself and aligning with the word of God.

Today is your long awaited moment of emancipation. Freedom is calling out for you. Answer it! Here's your chance to hit the reset button and start over fresh. Now is the time to let it all go.

Take an honest inventory of yourself. Clean out your emotional closet. Untether yourself from the pain. Let the peace of God rule in your heart. Accept the things that you cannot control. Surrender to your Heavenly Father all the burdens that you were never meant to carry. Give the world a shining biblical example of what real forgiveness looks like. Visualize and experience the layers of the past being lifted off of you one by one. Embrace the serenity of being whole again. You are now free!

Positive Affirmation:

I forgive myself and all those who have wronged me. I embrace the freedom of peace and walk in divine healing. The more I release, the more incredible I feel. I am free!!

Self-Assessment Questions:

Why did Jesus die on the cross?

Is there any unforgiveness in my heart that I need to address?

What is the difference between denial and true forgiveness?

Have I honestly forgiven the people who have wronged me or am I just in denial?

How amazing does it feel inside to release and let go?

How will forgiving others more quickly in the future improve my life?

What is the body language of a person who has forgiven?

Who in my life has shown me the best example of forgiveness?

What helps me forgive others so easily now?

Have I truly forgiven myself for the things I've done in the past?

How does God want me to see myself?

Why is my future worth more to me than holding unforgiveness in my heart?

How does being able to forgive myself and others empower me?

Does my relationship with God improve when I let go of the wrongs done to me by others?

> **Today's Prayer:**
> I pray, Father, for you to reveal to me any unforgiveness in my heart. Help me to address it and completely turn it over to you. Give me the strength to let go of the past and any other destructive emotions I've been carrying so that nothing gets in the way of our relationship in Jesus' name. Amen.

Success Quotes:

And whenever you stand praying, if you have anything against anyone, forgive him, that your Father in Heaven may also forgive you your trespasses. But if you do not forgive, neither will your Father in Heaven forgive your trespasses.
—Jesus Christ

Forgiveness is not an occasional act, it is a constant attitude.
—Martin Luther King Jr.

To be a Christian means to forgive the inexcusable because God has forgiven the inexcusable in you.
—C.S. Lewis

If we don't forgive ourselves for mistakes we've made—and everybody's made their choices, some worse than others—we'll never experience the good life God has in store.
—Joel Osteen

When you forgive, you love. And when you love, God's light shines upon you.
—Jon Krakauer

Resentment is like drinking poison and then hoping it will kill your enemies.
—Nelson Mandela

It is only when the mind is free from the old that it meets everything anew, and in that there is joy.
—Jiddu Krishnamurti

Forgiveness is the final form of love.
—Reinhold Niebuhr

Letting ourselves be forgiven is one of the most difficult healings we will undertake and one of the most fruitful.
—Stephen Levine

You cannot forgive just once, forgiveness is a daily practice.
—Sonia Rumzi

To be wronged is nothing, unless you continue to remember it.
—Confucius

Be the one who nurtures and builds. Be the one who has an understanding and a forgiving heart one who looks for the best in people. Leave people better than you found them.
—Marvin J. Ashton

Your Action Steps:
Take out a sheet of paper and write down the names of everyone who has ever hurt, offended, or betrayed you. Once you have done that, pray over your list of names and ask God to bless them tremendously in every aspect of their lives. Do this every day until you flush all the negative energy and ill will towards these people out of your system.

Inspiration For Victory:
This is the turning point, everything in your life is about to change. God is about to restore the lost years and reward you for your faithfulness!

— Day Two —
GET ALONE WITH GOD DAILY

Bible Verse:
Very early in the morning, while it was still dark, Jesus got up, left the house and went off to a solitary place, where he prayed.
Mark 1:35

There is no substitute nor alternative to spending time alone with God. If your goal is to be successful, you must develop the discipline to set time aside every day to enter into his presence. Your Heavenly Father has so many important things that he wants to share with you. When you get away from the distractions, He can speak directly to your heart about his plans for the future.

God desires more than anything else to have a close and intimate relationship with you. The only real way to accomplish this is to seek him regularly. Doing this allows your Father to establish a direct line of communication between the two of you. During your devotional time, make sure you are totally present and giving him your full attention. By going into the silence, you can better hear the whisper of the Almighty. Every time you seek his presence, your connection with him will grow stronger.

The Lord doesn't want you to merely set up a daily ritual where you just go through the motions. He longs for you to approach each day as a new opportunity to get to know him. Your creator loves you and always has your best interest at heart. He wants to guide your decisions so that he can place you in position to fulfill your destiny. God can see the whole picture, from beginning to end, which enables him to know exactly what you need to do to succeed. When you seek him, he can impart on you the wisdom and revelation needed to keep you out of trouble.

From cover to cover, the bible tells of great men retreating alone in order to pray, meditate, and commune with God. Following their examples will allow you to draw from his strength and replenish emotionally. In a world full of distractions, it can be very challenging to stay connected spiritually. Seeking times of silence will help quiet your mind and bring you back into focus. Every time you are detached from him you are vulnerable to making serious mistakes. This is the reason why it's so vital to stay plugged in daily.

Make every area of your life available to God. Each day, lay your cares and concerns at the feet of the one who has the answers. Sit back and just listen to the things he places in your heart. Surrender and submit to all his instructions. Let him fully prepare you for the amazing future he has laid out for you. Incorporating this principle into your life will impact you in unimaginable ways.

Positive Affirmation:

Every day, I spend time alone with the one who really loves me. From him, I draw my strength, wisdom, and peace. His spirit guides me in all my decisions and my life prospers because of it.

Self-Assessment Questions:

How much time am I spending alone with God?

Can you have a deep relationship with someone you never spend time with?

Why is it so important to get alone with God before making important decisions?

What time each day can I set aside to enter fully into his presence?

Do I consult with God when I face challenges or do I try to handle them on my own?

How would spending more time with God improve my life?

Do I give the Lord my full attention when I am alone with him?

Is there anything in my life that is hindering our relationship?

How often do I read God's word?

Is my alone time with God just a ritual or am I actually seeking his heart?

Do I stay connected to his spirit throughout the day or just in my alone time?

In what area of my life does God want me to make changes?

When in the past could I most feel God's presence?

Today's Prayer:

Lord, help me to establish a better relationship with you. Show me how to listen better so that I can understand your will for my future. Give me the strength to bring my concerns to you first before making any decisions. Help me establish set times every day to get alone with you in Jesus' name. Amen.

Success Quotes:

Spending time with God is the key to our strength and success in all areas of life. Be sure that you never try to work God into your schedule, but always work your schedule around Him.
—Joyce Meyer

The prayer closet is the arena which produces the overcomer.
—Paul E. Billheimer

We can be tired, weary and emotionally distraught, but after spending time alone with God, we find that He injects into our bodies energy, power and strength.
—Charles Stanley

Silence is the room we create for the searching of God, where we hear His voice and follow.
—Mark Buchanan

When you are in the dark, listen, and God will give you a very precious message.
—Oswald Chambers

Prayer is not monologue, but dialogue; God's voice is its most essential part. Listening to God's voice is the secret of the assurance that He will listen to mine.
—Andrew Murray

You may pray for an hour and still not pray. You may meet God for a moment and then be in touch with Him all day.
—Fredrik Wisloff

The Bible says, "Be still and know that I am God" (Psalm 46:10 NIV). That means sit down and shut up. That's how you hear God

and get near to God. You have to sit alone and just be quiet with your Bible and say, "God, is there anything you want to say to me?
—Rick Warren

When our quiet times have become hurried, how can we expect to give God the adoration that is His due? How can we receive the guidance that God is waiting to give? How can our hearts catch the glow of divine fire? How can we have deep fellowship with those purposes that are really nearest to the heart of God?
—Gordon M. Guinness

But thou, when thou prayest, enter into thy closet, and when thou hast shut thy door, pray to thy Father which is in secret; and thy Father which seeth in secret shall reward thee openly.
—Matthew 6:6

Your Action Steps:
Set aside at least fifteen minutes every day to be alone with God. Spend the first five minutes praying for others, the next five minutes thanking God for meeting all your needs, and the last five minutes just listening. The more you do this, the more revelation God will give you about his plans for your life.

Inspiration For Victory:
God has amazing things he wants to share with you. The more you get alone with him, the more he can use you to accomplish his purposes!

— Day Three —
ADOPT THE MINDSET OF THE UNSTOPPABLE

Bible Verse:
We demolish arguments and every pretension that sets itself up against the knowledge of God, and we take captive every thought to make it obedient to Christ.
2 Corinthians 10:5

Having big dreams, goals, and ambitions is awesome. Shooting for the stars is a step towards greatness. However, it's one thing to aim high, it's another thing to be able to do it.

What separates champions from the rest is that they are mentally wired differently. They have a belief system that sees failures and setbacks as just part of the process towards achieving success.

Winners absolutely hate losing. They despise every ounce of the experience, but this doesn't mean they are bad sports when life doesn't go as planned. True champions are always gracious and respectful in defeat because they frame it properly. They know how to anchor the emotions of a loss and convert it into motivation, becoming even more hungry and determined to succeed. On the days the will to train is not there, they tap back into that pain of defeat and feed off it.

Champions understand what gives them the advantage is their mindset. They discipline and condition their mind to do the impossible. For you to turn your dreams into reality, you're going to have to master the psychology of winning. Day in and day out you must conquer the battlefield of the mind. Refuse to entertain self-limiting beliefs in any way shape or form. Carry yourself differently, prepare differently, and most of all see failure differently.

To become unstoppable you must constantly have the inner soundtrack of victory blaring from your spirit. Super achievers maintain a growth mindset which empowers them to see pain, losses, and setbacks as learning opportunities. Never look at defeat as permanent, but rather see it as temporary gestation period from which a greater victory will be born.

Winning is a mindset. Success involves taking risks and being able to function outside the comfort zone. Destiny is a journey that consists of ups and downs. Sometimes life's going to hit you with a brick, and when it does your mindset will either make you or break you. You're a champion and champions don't lay down, they don't let up, and most of all they never give up. By adopting the paradigm of the unstoppable, temporary defeat will be no match for you.

Positive Affirmation:

I choose to see and frame all defeats as temporary. Each day I will learn and expand with divine revelation. Step by step I will grow into the successful person I aim to become.

Self-Assessment Questions:

In what areas of my life do I most need to grow?

Am I willing to continue pursing my goals even when I fail?

What is the mindset of a champion?

Do I currently have the paradigm (belief system) that it takes to be successful?

Who do I know that has a wining mindset?

How does a successful person respond to a loss?

Do I become more determined or do I shut down when things don't go my way?

How can I use losing to motivate me to push even harder?

When in the past did I apply a growth mindset to overcome a challenge?

Why is learning from my mistakes so vital to my success?

Do I see failure as permanent or temporary?

In what ways can I grow and expand my talents?

How can I improve my life today?

Today's Prayer:
I pray today, Father, for a growth mindset. Help me see obstacles, setbacks, and losses as a learning process. I submit all my beliefs to you. Assist me in mentally framing each experience in a proper and constructive way for my own improvement in Jesus' name. Amen.

Success Quotes:

History has demonstrated that the most notable winners usually encountered heart-breaking obstacles before they triumphed. They won because they refused to become discouraged by their defeats.
—B.C. Forbes

Many of life's failures are people who did not realize how close they were to success when they gave up.
—Thomas Edison

Failure is not fatal, but failing to change might be.
—John Wooden

I don't divide the world into the weak and the strong, or the successes and the failures... I divide the world into the learners and the non-learners.
—Benjamin Barber

I hated every minute of training, but I said, 'Don't quit. Suffer now and live the rest of your life as a champion.
—Muhammad Ali

The last three or four reps is what makes the muscle grow. This area of pain divides the champion from someone else who is not a champion. That's what most people lack, having the guts to go on and just say they'll go through the pain no matter what happens.
—Arnold Schwarzenegger

There's a difference in thinking you are a champion and knowing that you are.
—Matthew McConaughey

Life's not about how hard of a hit you can give... it's about how many you can take, and still keep moving forward.
—Sylvester Stallone (Rocky Balboa)

Most of the important things in the world have been accomplished by people who have kept on trying when there seemed no hope at all.

—Dale Carnegie

Would you like me to give you a formula for success? It's quite simple, really. Double your rate of failure.
—Thomas Watson

How you think when you lose determines how long it will be until you win.
—Gilbert Keith Chesterton

It's not that I'm so smart, it's just that I stay with problems longer.
—Albert Einstein

If parents want to give their children a gift, the best thing they can do is to teach their children to love challenges, be intrigued by mistakes, enjoy effort, and keep on learning.
—Carol Dweck

Anyone can train to be a gladiator. What marks you out is having the mindset of a champion.
—Manu Bennett

A challenge only becomes an obstacle when you bow to it.
—Ray A. Davis

The mind is a powerful thing. It can take you through walls.
—Denis Avey

You may have to fight a battle more than once to win it.
—Margaret Thatcher

Your Action Steps:
To fulfill God's destiny for your life you must reprogram your mind! Each day from here forward make it a point of emphasis to watch positive motivational videos, listen to self help audio programs, and read inspirational material that will help you stay focused on success. The object here is to pour so much positivity into your mind that there's no room for anything else.

Inspiration For Victory:
The Lord, who is mighty in all things, dares you to trust him with your dreams!

— Day Four —
DEFINE YOUR CORE VALUES

Bible Verse:
But the fruit of the Spirit is love, joy, peace, patience, kindness, goodness, faithfulness, gentleness, self-control; against such things there is no law.
Galatians 5:2-23

Just like the world's tallest skyscrapers, success must be built on a deep and solid foundation. Enduring prosperity can only be engineered with solid core values, strong righteous principles, and impeccable character. These three universal elements are timeless. They are the steel, concrete, and trusses that hold it all together. Building on a corrupt foundation will jeopardize the whole structure. If not properly addressed, it can and will bring your tower down.

Your core values dictate your behavior and attitude in all situations. They are the personal code that you represent and choose to live by. These values, embodied together, govern every aspect of your life. They become the filtering principles of every action and decision you make. What you do consistently will define your character, articulate what you stand for, and clarify who you really are.

Christian values are the time proven ingredients God gave you to build your life around. These are the bricks and reinforced columns designed to support the highest levels of achievement. Talent can take you to the top, but it's your character that has to keep you there. It's the difference between leasing and actually owning success. Every time you sow the seeds of God's universal truth you strengthen your success infrastructure.

To walk in the fullness of your destiny you must get the core right, for without it, nothing else matters. Today mediatate on the values that are most important for you to constantly exemplify like honesty, integrity, love, truth, loyalty, discipline, compassion, responsibility, impacting others, etc. Bring all your thoughts, words, and actions into alignment with them. Let these core principles become your new way of life.

Be a person who stands for something. Refuse to compromise or be swayed by emotions. External circumstances should never dictate your actions, it's who you are at the core that should always command your responses. Judge your life not by how much you can achieve or accumulate, but rather by the level to which you stay true to yourself. Filter all your decisions through biblical principles and never sacrifice your character no matter what the price.

> **Positive Affirmation:**
> I know who I am and what I stand for. My character is impeccable, my core is solid, and I live my life through strong righteous principles.

Self-Assessment Questions:

What are my top seven core values?

What word best describes who I am at my core?

What value do I want to most represent to others?

What are the principles that I most admire in others?

What kind of character is most important for a strong leader to display?

What principles do all successful people seem to have in common?

What is my life going to look like when I consistently live through my core values?

How does it feel to be a person of high character?

What morale values are most important to my family?
What kind of character do I look for in my friends and associates?
What are the most important business principles?
What values do I want my soul mate to represent?
What principles do I want my children to emulate?

> **Today's Prayer:**
> Father, today I pray for you to show me any flaws in my character. Help me to build my life on a solid foundation so that I can represent you with credibility. Thank you for tearing down anything in me that is not strong enough to support enduring success in Jesus' name. Amen.

Success Quotes:

For what shall it profit a man, if he shall gain the whole world, and lose his own soul?
—Mark 8:36

The ability to subordinate an impulse to a value is the essence of the proactive person. Reactive people are driven by feelings, by circumstances, by conditions, by their environment. Proactive people are driven by values - carefully thought about, selected and internalized values.
—Stephen Covey

The supreme quality for leadership is unquestionably integrity. Without it, no real success is possible, no matter whether it is on a section gang, a football field, in an army, or in an office.
—Dwight D. Eisenhower

Your beliefs become your thoughts, Your thoughts become your words, Your words become your actions, Your actions become your habits, Your habits become your values, Your values become your destiny.
—Mahatma Gandhi

It's not hard to make decisions when you know what your values are.
—Roy Disney

"The first principle of value that we need to rediscover is this: that all reality hinges on moral foundations. In other words, that this is a moral universe, and that there are moral laws of the universe just as abiding as the physical laws.
—Martin Luther King Jr.

To be mature you have to realize what you value most... Not to arrive at a clear understanding of one's own values is a tragic waste. You have missed the whole point of what life is for.
—Eleanor Roosevelt

The intelligent have plans; the wise have principles.
—Raheel Farooq

True leaders don't look at just the outward appearances in the selection of team members, they look at one's core values and heart.
—Farshad Asl

Trust is the glue of life. It's the most essential ingredient in effective communication. It's the foundational principle that holds all relationships.
—Stephen Covey

Your Action Steps:
Write down the 7 core values that mean the most to you personally (For example: wisdom, truth, faith, love, peace, kindness, excellence, etc.). The things on this list should be what you want your life to stand for and what you most want your life to represent. Once you have your core values written out, examine each area of your life to make sure you are in alignment with them. From this point forward, filter all your life decisions through this list.

Inspiration For Victory:
God's hand is on your life and you are about to ascend to greater heights than you could ever imagine!

— Day Five —
CREATE A POWERFUL VISION

Bible Verse:
Where there is no vision, the people perish: but he that keepeth the law, happy is he.
Proverbs 29:18

Vision is the genesis of all greatness. It's your destiny foreseen in the mental realm before actualization. Success must be first engineered in the mind. Your imagination is the womb that will give birth to your future. The starting point of personal transformation is developing a powerful mental blueprint with the exact specifications for how you desire your life to look. Doing this will clarify your intentions, bring you into focus, and separate you from 99% of the world.

The blessed and unstoppable think differently. They are mental architects that imagine and design with their mind the kind of world they want to live in. Through visualization, these innovators construct and assemble the storyboard of their future. Pioneers understand that the world is pliable, and with enough mental clarity they can bend and shape their future at will. They don't need eyes, they see with their mind. These stubborn dreamers wrestle with reality until reality taps out and gives them precisely what they want.

People with gigantic dreams become magnetic. Having a strong vision for your own future will attract the right people and circumstances needed to bring itself into fruition. Anything you can envision clear enough and long enough, you can make happen.

Those without a vision walk through life in a state of confusion. Champions understand that success doesn't materialize by chance or randomness but rather by strategic thought and purposed intent. Before you can build the life of your dreams, you must predetermine your outcomes. Do some real soul searching as to what you want to be a part of, and what you want to build during your time here on earth. Decide exactly who it is that you want to be, where you wish to go, and what you desire to accomplish?

Your assignment with this principle is to establish in your mind a clear picture of your ultimate desired state. Develop a vision that inspires and motivates you to become the best person that you can be. Let it become your so called "North Star" that guides your every decision. All your goals and objectives should move you in some way towards bringing this vision alive.

Imagine grand outcomes for your life as if there were no limitations or barriers to restrict you from achieving them. Think outside of the box by moving your mind into the realm of unlimited possibilities. Begin the construction now. Create in your mind today the world that you want to see in the future.

Positive Affirmation:

My life is being brought into divine order. The vision I have for my life overwhelms me with inspiration. Circumstances and events are being set in motion right now for me to accomplish everything I see so vividly in mind.

Self-Assessment Questions:

What do I desire most in life?

Who do I really want to be?

How do I define true success?

What do I want my body to look and feel like?

What kind of marriage do I want to have?

What do I want to accomplish in the future?

How can I make the biggest impact with my life?

What would make me feel most alive inside?

What kind of personal relationships am I looking for?

How do I want the world to see me?

Are my dreams and desires in line with God's word?

How will getting clear on what I want drastically improve my life?

What does success really feel like?

How can I make the image of my future more vivid and clear in my mind?

What area of my life currently has the most clarity?

What area of my life has the least?

Today's Prayer:

Thank you, Father, for giving me a clear vision for each area of my life. Give me the strength to keep that image of your plan in my mind with full expectation that it will come to pass in Jesus' name. Amen.

Success Quotes:

The most pathetic person in the world is someone who has sight but no vision.
—Hellen Keller

The first step toward creating an improved future is developing the ability to envision it. VISION will ignite the fire of passion that fuels our commitment to do WHATEVER IT TAKES to achieve excellence. Only VISION allows us to transform dreams of greatness into the reality of achievement through human action. VISION has no boundaries and knows no limits. Our VISION is what we become in life.
—Tony Dungy

The best way to succeed is to have a specific Intent, a clear Vision, a plan of Action, and the ability to maintain Clarity. Those are the Four Pillars of Success. It never fails!
—Steve Maraboli

Good business leaders create a vision, articulate the vision, passionately own the vision, and relentlessly drive it to completion.
—Jack Welch

Vision without an Action is Illusion. Action without a Vision is Confusion.
—Sunny John

The most valuable people in the world are "Visionary People"
—Amit Kalantri

That's been one of my mantras - focus and simplicity. Simple can be harder than complex: You have to work hard to get your thinking clean to make it simple. But it's worth it in the end, because once you get there, you can move mountains.
—Steve Jobs

Your heart is able to see things that your eyes aren't able to.
—Kholoud Yasser

All successful people men and women are big dreamers. They imagine what their future could be, ideal in every respect, and then they work every day toward their distant vision, that goal or purpose.
—Brian Tracy

A leader has the vision and conviction that a dream can be achieved. He inspires the power and energy to get it done.
—Ralph Lauren

Dissatisfaction and discouragement are not caused by the absence of things, but the absence of vision.
—Anonymous

> **Your Action Steps:**
> Today envision how you want each area of your life to look (health, family, marriage, relationships, and finances, etc.). Examine your desires to verify that they are all in align with God's word, then paint these outcomes onto the mental canvas of your mind. Make the image so real that you can grab it with both hands and pull it into the present. Let your imagination place you in the center of your future so that you can experience every sensation fully in the now. Lock these vivid images into your mind and revisit them daily until they materialize.

> **Inspiration For Victory:**
> **When you see the world from a kingdom persepctive your options are unlimited, for with God ALL things are possible!**

— Day Six —
FOLLOW YOUR PASSION

Bible Verse:
For the gifts and the calling of God are irrevocable.
Romans 11:29

The secret to success is building your life around doing the things you love. Excellence is impossible to attain without a burning desire to achieve it. This motivation comes from doing work that you enjoy and are personally connected to. Enthusiasm gives you an edge that allows you to perform at a higher level than your competition. When passion is married to a singleness of purpose it produces the environment needed for greatness.

God has given you specific interests that are required for your anointed calling. When choosing a career path, never sacrifice your passion simply for a job that pays more money. People that make career decisions this way become entrenched in professions that ultimately leave them unfulfilled. Working forty hours or more a week, doing a job God never designed you to do, will only make you miserable. For you to thrive, you must do the things that make you feel alive.

Your passion points to your divine calling. Acknowledge the flames that blaze on the inside of you and allow them to fully express themselves. The more you do the things that excite you, the more the opportunities will arise for you to continue to do them. Your expertise, your talents, and your zeal for doing what you love will open all the doors needed to succeed in life.

Chasing your dreams is the way to discovering your own identity. Pour all your time and energy into the things that you are obsessed with. In the beginning, don't focus on the compensation. Your main concern should be finding the ideal environment to sharpen your skills. Day after day, just keep perfecting your craft until you master the gifts your creator gave you.

Passion is the intense energy created when one is doing what God designed them to do. To achieve greatness you must align with something that allows you to fully harness that power. Refuse to settle for an occupation that doesn't set you on fire. The only way to find your own voice is to do what you love. You'll never go wrong when you dream big, follow your heart, and chase your passion!

> **Positive Affirmation:**
> I commit today to moving towards my passion. Inside, I feel the most alive when I am passionately doing the things I love. Each day I will perfect my craft until I can do it full time.

Self-Assessment Questions:

What makes me feel alive on the inside?

What really sparks my creativity?

What job or profession would I be willing to do whether I got paid or not?

What are some of my favorite topics of conversation?

What was the last thing I can remember doing that I totally lost track of time?

If money wasn't an issue, what profession or cause would I get involved in?

What's my favorite section in the bookstore?

If I could do one thing to change the world today what would it be?

What would be my top three dream jobs?

If I could start my own business today what would it be?

What three skills do I possess that I love and enjoy to do?

What would I need to change in order to do my passion full time?

What's the worst thing that could happen if I pursued my passion full speed?

Which is more important to me avoiding failure or living out my dreams?

Today's Prayer:
Thank you, Father, for the interests and passions you have planted in my spirit. Help me to find more and more opportunities where I can flourish using them in Jesus' name.

Success Quotes:

I think I overcame every single one of my personal shortcomings by the sheer passion I brought to my work. If you love your work, you'll be out there every day trying to do it the best you possibly can, and pretty soon everybody around will catch the passion from you—like a fever.
—Sam Walton

If you want to be successful in a particular field of endeavor, I think perseverance is one of the key qualities. It's very important that you find something that you care about, that you have a deep passion for, because you're going to have to devote a lot of your life to it.
—George Lucas

When you set yourself on fire, people love to come and see you burn.
—John Wesley

The one thing that you have that nobody else has is you. Your voice, your mind, your story, your vision. So write and draw and build and play and dance and live as only you can.
—Neil Gaiman

The most wonderful thing in the world is somebody who knows who they are…and knows what they were created to do.
Bishop T.D. Jakes

You have to be burning with an idea, or a problem, or a wrong that you want to right. If you're not passionate enough from the start, you'll never stick it out.
—Steve Jobs

Don't ask yourself what the world needs; ask yourself what makes you come alive. And then go and do that. Because what the world needs is people who have come alive.
—Howard Thurman

One person with passion is better than forty people merely interested.
—E. M. Forster

One of the things that may get in the way of people…is that they're not in touch with their passion. If you're passionate about what it is you do, then you're going to be looking for everything you can to get better at it.
—Jack Canfield

Your Action Steps:
Today lay out an effective strategy to replace your current income so that you can do your passion full time. Set a timeline of 3-6 months to achieve this. Your objective is to structure your life in a way that will allow you to apply all your focus and energy towards doing the things you love.

Inspiration For Victory:
The Lord works in remarkable ways. Trust him to break down every wall or obstacle that stands in your way!

—Day Seven—
AWAKEN TO YOUR CALLING

Bible Verse:
Wherefore also we pray always for you, that our God would count you worthy of this calling, and fulfil all the good pleasure of his goodness, and the work of faith with power:
2 Thessalonians 1:11

The day that you discover your life's calling will be the turning point in your life. God will shake Heaven and Earth to move you towards this discovery. If you don't know right now what that calling is, start spending time alone with him. Pray for his guidance and direction over your life. Revelation will come in his perfect timing. It could happen in the silence when you least expect it, or it could make itself known through some dark life experience. Your heavenly Father will speak in whatever way or language needed for you to understand what he wants you to do.

Once you awaken to his purpose, the Holy Spirit will start to align circumstances and events to help you launch your mission. A powerful dream will begin to arise on the inside of you giving your life a whole new sense of meaning. Let him show you exactly who he made you to be. Yield to his guidance so that he can maneuver you into the center of your assignment.

God's purpose for your life will always align with his word. He has anointed you with a set of unique talents for a reason. His calling for your life will be directly tied to using these abilities. The world needs exactly what he has planted inside of you and only you can deliver it. He will set up divine appointments with influential people to confirm your calling. These chosen vessels will inspire and encourage you to boldly move forward.

Chasing a goal is only relevant if it is rooted in the fulfillment of God's plan. Your vision for your life must be God's vision or you will be ultimately working in vain. Functioning outside of his calling gives birth to disillusionment, frustration, and spiritual emptiness. Striving for the things of God will bring about a level of peace that surpasses all understanding. Always remember this, if there's no peace in your heart for what you are doing that's a clear sign that God's not in it.

When you know in your spirit that God has chosen you to do something, it emboldens you to act in a manner that makes you unstoppable. Nothing can stand in the way of God's incredible plans for your future. You will face many trials and troubles along the way, but by faithfully trusting God you will overcome!

Positive Affirmation:

I was not made by mistake, I was intentionally designed to fulfill a divine calling. God has an amazing purpose for my life! By following the spirit of peace, I will arrive at the center of his wonderful plan.

Self-Assessment Questions:

What special talents and abilities has God given me?

When do I feel the most alive?

How can I use my passions, talents, and values to make the world better?

What are some of the life challenges and difficulties that I had to overcome?

In what ways could I help other people do the same?

When I was a child what was I really passionate about?

What are some of the world causes that I strongly connect with?

What am I doing when I feel the most at peace?

What are some of the dreams and goals God has planted in me?

When do I feel the most authentic?

If I could convey a message to the world what would it be?

What can I do right now that would begin to prepare me for my calling?

How great would it feel to be doing God's special purpose?

In what ways can I use my talents to expand the kingdom of God?

Today's Prayer:

Thank you father for choosing me for your special calling. Help me to be patient as you guide me towards full revelation of this purpose. I surrender to your perfect timing knowing that you have my best interest at heart in Jesus' name. Amen.

Success Quotes:

If you ask me what I came to do in this world, I, an artist, will answer you: I am here to live out loud.
—Émile Zola

I believe there's a calling for all of us. I know that every human being has value and purpose. The real work of our lives is to become aware. And awakened. To answer the call.
—Oprah Winfrey

If God gives you something you can do, why in God's name wouldn't you do it?
—Stephen King

I have brought myself by long meditation to the conviction that a human being with a settled purpose must accomplish it, and that nothing can resist a will which will stake even existence upon its fulfillment.
—Benjamin Disraeli

When faith replaces doubt, when selfless service eliminates selfish striving, the power of God brings to pass His purposes.
—Thomas S. Monson

The mystery of human existence lies not in just staying alive, but in finding something to live for.
—Fyodor Dostoyevsky

The purpose of life is to contribute in some way to making things better.
—Robert F. Kennedy

You didn't create yourself, so there is no way you can tell yourself what you were created for! If I handed you an invention you had never seen before, you wouldn't know its purpose, and the invention itself wouldn't be able to tell you either. Only the creator or the owner's manual could reveal its purpose.
—Rick Warren

Be a lamp, or a lifeboat, or a ladder. Help someone's soul heal. Walk out of your house like a shepherd.
—Rumi

The purpose of life is not to be happy—but to matter, to be productive, to be useful, to have it make some difference that you lived at all.
—Leo Rosten

Your Action Steps:
There's a special kind of environment needed for your divine calling to reveal itself. If your life is disorganized and full of chaos there's no room for your true purpose to bloom. The key to awakening to your assignment is to master where you are at. The way to do this is to create balance and order in every aspect of your life. It's time to declutter, get organized, and cultivate an atmosphere of absolute harmony. Establishing this kind of peace and stillness will silence the worldly distractions and allow you to become more aware of your inner voice.

Inspiration For Victory:
The Lord is directing your steps to victory, all you have to do is follow him!

— Day Eight —
SPEAK THE LANGUAGE OF HEAVEN

Bible Verse:
Now faith is the substance of things hoped for, the evidence of things not seen.
Hebrews 11:1

Faith is the oxygen that breathes life into your dreams. It's the process of seeing and believing in the future state of something without any evidence or assurance to prove it. Although you cannot see or experience your dream yet in the physical, you must still align your every thought, word, and action with the full expectation of it materializing. To walk in the fullness of the blessing one must understand that begging doesn't move God, faith does. When you speak with complete certainty, when you walk with absolute confidence, when you operate with bold anticipation you create a powerful presence of undeniable influence. Functioning with this type of trust and conviction makes all things possible.

Destiny is obligated, by universal law, to concede to the demands of unwavering faith. The level that you receive will always be equivalent to the level of your belief. Your vision for the future needs corresponding expectation in order to bring it alive. A dream without faith behind it is just an impotent wish. Only what you truly believe is yours, will you ever possess.

Others might not be able to see or understand your vision, because destiny hides itself in the mind of the one who will inherit it. In order to receive this inheritance you must protect your faith at all times, especially in the beginning stages. The world will attempt to inject and impregnate you with a deadly disease called doubt. This contagious cancer is a dream killer set on murdering your future.

You must destroy, annihilate, and uproot all traces of it from your life. Faith never accepts or entertains any other outcome than the one believed for.

Close the door of your inner circle to anyone that does not believe in your dreams. Quarantine the naysayers around you, limit their access, and refuse to let them infect your mind. Surround yourself with super believers, prayer warriors, and people who will come into agreement with you for your aspirations.

Unwavering faith moves mountains. When understood and properly applied it becomes a catalyst for change. Every miracle Jesus performed he used the law of faith to do it. Believers have access to this same power, and with Jesus interceding on their behalf, can do even greater wonders.

Faith is the only language spoken in heaven, therefore it's the only language the universe yields to. Belief is the chosen tongue that releases the blessing, so the quality of your future depends on how fluent you become in it. When expectation and dreams collide they explode with manifestation. Faith pulls dreams from the imaginary and thrusts them into reality. Whatever it is that you desire to do or become, anticipate it coming to complete fruition and it will. Hold on to your vision with both hands and never let it go.

Positive Affirmation:

I walk in pure faith knowing that what I have envisioned for my life will come to pass. I am submitted, sold out, and all in committed to achieving the fulfillment of my God given assignment. I will not be denied!

Self-Assessment Questions:

What does having faith really mean to me?

What's the difference between having real faith and just hoping something will happen?

In what areas of my life am I currently showing expectation?

How will believing in myself more change my life?

Who do I know that most represents faith in their lives?

Who are the biggest dream killers and doubters around me?

How can I limit their access to my mind?

Who are my biggest supporters in life?

Who encourages me most to chase my dreams?

Do I fully believe in my heart that I can accomplish my goals?

What areas of my life do I need to apply more faith?

What's the body language of someone who really believes their going to succeed?

When in my past did I most exemplify unwavering faith?

What's the difference between faith and trust?

Today's Prayer:
Father, I pray that you would raise my faith to a level that you can work your miracles through. Thank you for strengthening my belief in you. Help me to cultivate a spirit of expectation so that I can fulfill the purpose that you called me to do. May your mighty name be glorified in everything I accomplish in Jesus' name. Amen.

Success Quotes:

All I have seen teaches me to trust the Creator for all I have not seen.
—Ralph Waldo Emerson

Faith is taking the first step even when you don't see the whole staircase.
—Martin Luther King, Jr.

For we walk by faith, not by sight.
—2 Corinthians 5:7

To one who has faith, no explanation is necessary. To one without faith, no explanation is possible.
—St. Thomas Aquinas

In faith there is enough light for those who want to believe and enough shadows to blind those who don't.
—Blaise Pascal

Oh, brethren, be great believers! Little faith will bring your souls to heaven, but great faith will bring heaven to you.
—C.H. Spurgeon

I would rather err on the side of faith than on the side of doubt.
—Robert Schuller

Feed your faith and your fears will starve to death.
—Unknown

Faith activates God - Fear activates the Enemy.
—Joel Osteen

Because you have so little faith. Truly I tell you, if you have faith as small as a mustard seed, you can say to this mountain, 'Move from here to there,' and it will move. Nothing will be impossible for you.
—Jesus Christ

Faith is to believe what you do not see; the reward of this faith is to see what you believe.
—Saint Augustine

Therefore I tell you, whatever you ask for in prayer, believe that you have received it, and it will be yours.
—Mark 11:24

Your Action Steps:
1. Pray for God to help you with your unbelief.
2. Immerse yourself in the word of God. (Read, Listen, and Watch Bible orientated programs every day.)
3. Study the lives of those who have achieved great things due to their unwaivering faith.
4. Begin to distance yourself from anyone that casts doubt on you achieving your dream.
5. Stay around people who inspire and encourage you to pursue your calling.

Inspiration For Victory:
You are a child of the most high God, the modern day Goliaths are no match for you!

— Day Nine —
FIND YOUR WHY

Bible Verse:
All the ways of man are pure in his own eyes, but the Lord weighs the spirit.
Proverbs 16:2

What's your "why"? Why do you want to be successful? Whatever you truly crave and aspire to accomplish needs to be dissected and deeply understood. Your "why" is not the ultimate goal you are striving for, it's the motivation behind it and why you desire it in the first place. It's the purpose, cause, or belief that motivates you to want to be successful. There will be numerous trials and tribulations throughout life, your "why" is the vehicle that will carry you through them.

The higher the level of success that you wish to experience, the stronger your "why" must be. Only when you develop an undeniable motivation to achieve something will you ever achieve it. Anything can be accomplished if there's a good enough reason behind doing it. Whatever it takes to put yourself into the mindset of I won't be denied, do it. Nothing can stop a person who has no other choice but to succeed.

Your motives are the rocket fuel that thrust your dreams into orbit. The last thing you want to do is run out of gas midflight. Champions know inside why they want what they want, and that "why" takes them to the promise land. They tap into a cause that motivates them and a belief that inspires them to go beyond just being good. It's what pushes them to consistently outwork the competition and to stick it out during the turbulent times. The why is the birthplace of champions. She is the mother to all the legends and greats in every field. Whether it's a corporation, family, team, marriage, or an individual, each one of them needs a strong enough "why" to make it.

Make sure all your desires are built around righteousness. Filter all your motives and intentions through the fruits of the Spirit which are love, joy, peace, patience, kindness, goodness, faithfulness, gentleness, self-control; against such things there is no law. Motives rooted in revenge are self-destructive and will ultimately hinder your success. Never make your "why" dependent on anyone or anything external. If you do, your "why" will be left vulnerable if outside circumstances or situations change.

The success journey must be traveled day in and day out, so if what your doing doesn't wake you up early and keep you up late then you need to do something else. If you feel stuck or seem to be lacking motivation, examine your reasons for doing it in the first place. You need to feel connected to what it is you are doing, because all your energy flows out of that connection. The more deeply you are connected to the thing you are doing the more likely you will accomplish it. Find the motive that ignites you on the inside and make that the centerpiece of your life. Awaken to your own why and you will be destined for greatness.

Positive Affirmation:

I am highly motivated and committed to living a life of success. I have honest and pure motives that drive me every day. I know what I want and why I want it. I will not be denied!

Self-Assessment Questions:

Why do I really want to be successful in life?

How strong is my why?

In what areas do I need to be more honest with myself?

What drives successful people to be great?

How does it feel inside to be really motivated?

Who is the most motivated person I know?

What's their why?

What does it mean to me if I fail?

Is my why strong enough to pull me through trials and tribulations?

What belief drives me to do what I do?

What are the motives behind me wanting what I want?

When in the past did I have the wrong motives behind my actions?

How deeply am I connected to my purpose?

Is my why now pure and in line with my values?

Today's Prayer:

Father, I pray that you would help me examine my why behind the things I desire in life. Help me to address any internal motives that are out of line with you. Purify my intentions so that I can walk in a way that pleases you in Jesus' name. Amen.

Success Quotes:

Wanting something is not enough. You must hunger for it. Your motivation must be absolutely compelling in order to overcome the obstacles that will invariably come your way.
—Les Brown

When you want to succeed as bad as you want to breathe you will be successful.
—Eric Thomas

He who has a why to live for can bear almost any how.
—Friedrich Nietzsche

There are two great days in a person's life - the day we are born and the day we discover why.
—William Barclay

Nothing shocks me anymore...except pure intentions.
—Donna Lynn Hope

Men (people) are rarely aware of the real reasons which motivate their actions.
—Edward L. Bernays

The moment there is suspicion about a person's motives, everything he does becomes tainted.
—Mohandas Gandhi

A gift consists not in what is done or given, but in the intention of the giver or doer.
—Seneca

Power is not alluring to pure minds.
—Thomas Jefferson

Great thoughts and a pure heart, that is what we should ask from God.
—Johann Wolfgang von Goethe

My strength is as the strength of ten, because my heart is pure.
—Alfred Lord Tennyson

People don't buy what you do; they buy why you do it. And what you do simply proves what you believe.
—Simon Sinek

Talent is a wonderful thing, but it won't carry a quitter.
—Stephen King

Your Action Steps:

1. Write down 10 powerful reasons why you want to be successful.
2. Narrow this list down to the top three that motivate and inspire you the most.
3. Write those down on a separate business or index card. Now you have your WHY. Carry it with you wherever you go. Whenever things get hard in life, pull out your WHY and let it remind you of the reasons you must keep pushing forward.

Inspiration For Victory:

Tell your problems and difficulties how small they look standing next to God!

— Day Ten —
RAISE YOUR STANDARD

Bible Verse:
This Daniel became distinguished above all the other presidents and satraps, because an excellent spirit was in him. And the king planned to set him over the whole kingdom.
Daniel 6:3

Success is a marathon of consistency walked out one day at a time. Winners are constantly competing against themselves striving to get better. They are way too busy focusing on their execution and output to be concerned with the scoreboard. In their mind, good is the enemy of great, anything less than phenomenal is not an option. By trusting, pursuing, and perfecting the process that wins championships, they actually get to possess them.

Excellence is transportation. She's an elevator that can take you from the absolute bottom to the highest level imaginable. Wealth and prosperity have always had a love affair with her. She is magnetic, beautifully unmistakable, and universally recognized by everyone. There's no substitute or equivalent to her. When she enters the room everyone knows it.

People who hold themselves to an internal standard of greatness, regardless of the external circumstances, become the real difference makers of the world. Superior quality, high performance, and top notch service transcend all fads. They are the enduring and unquestionable ingredients that stand the test of time. All the great legends understood this and you can see it at every level of their work.

Success is the process of consistently doing the things that matter in an outstanding way. It's crucial to your ascension that you build a solid reputation for doing the ordinary exceptionally well. To become a champion you must cultivate a spirit of excellence until it becomes your way of life. Executing the fundamentals with precision, day in and day out, will enable you to climb to the top.

Greatness is an energy that rises and those that attach themselves to it will rise with it. Your daily focus should be on perfecting the basics in whatever field you are in. This is not about competition, this is about you being a good steward of the talents and abilities that God gave you. You were made in the image of the creator, so whatever you do should be done with a standard that truly honors him.

Mediocrity has no place in the life of a champion. Hold yourself accountable to the highest level of existence. Raise the bar and refuse to get complacent. Despise anything of average existence and have no association with it. The turning point in your life will be when you expect more from yourself than the world expects of you. When you do this, all the treasures and riches of the world will become available to you.

> **Positive Affirmation:**
>
> In everything I do I hold myself to the highest standard of excellence. I surround myself with people who understand its importance. I consistently do the right things the right way building an undeniable reputation for greatness.

Self-Assessment Questions:

What kind of standard am I holding myself to?

What does excellence mean to me?

In what ways can I improve my level of performance?

How would raising my level and quality of work improve my circumstances?

Who around me is currently performing at a level of greatness?

Am I more focused on the results or the process that brings those results about?

Who could I surround myself with that believes in the spirit of excellence?

Why is giving my best so important to me?

What am I saying to the world when I do not give my best?

Who is the person I most admire for their commitment to excellence?

Do I hold myself to the same standard when people aren't watching as I do when they are?

When has not performing at my best cost me?

What businesses, products, or brands represent excellence?

Who best exemplifies greatness in sports?

What can I learn from them?

Today's Prayer:

Lord, I pray today for you to give me the strength to give my all in everything. Help me to make excellence my new way of life. Give me the discipline to do my best even when people aren't watching so that I can honor you in all that I do in Jesus' name. Amen.

Success Quotes:

If a man is called to be a street sweeper, he should sweep streets even as a Michelangelo painted, or Beethoven composed music or Shakespeare wrote poetry. He should sweep streets so well that all the hosts of heaven and earth will pause to say, 'Here lived a great street sweeper who did his job well.
—Martin Luther King Jr.

If you don't have time to do it right, when will you have the time to do it over?
—John Wooden

Excellence is the Result of Caring more than others think is Wise, Risking more than others think is Safe, Dreaming more than others think is Practical, and Expecting more than others think is Possible.
—Ronnie Oldham

Excellence is to do a common thing in an uncommon way.
—Booker T. Washington

We don't get a chance to do that many things, and everyone should be really excellent. Because this is our life.
—Steve Jobs

Perfection is not attainable, but if we chase perfection we can catch excellence.
—Vince Lombardi

Excellence is an art won by training and habituation. We do not act rightly because we have virtue or excellence, but we rather have those because we have acted rightly. We are what we repeatedly do. Excellence, then, is not an act but a habit.
—Aristotle

The quality of a man's life is in direct proportion to his commitment to excellence, regardless of his chosen field of endeavor.
—Sherman Alexie

Excellence results from the accumulation of proper choices compounded over time.
—Orrin Woodward

Excellence is not a skill, it's an attitude.
—Ralph Marston

Excellence always sells.
—Earl Nightingale

Your Action Steps:
Write down one thing that you can do this week that will help you drastically improve each area of your life (health/marriage/relationships/family/finances/job or business/spiritual life). Once you have clarified the actions needed, schedule them in your planner so that you actually follow through with doing them. Focus on bringing your whole life into a state of excellence. If do this step for the next 12 weeks straight, unbelievable things will begin to happen to you!

Inspiration For Victory:
God's grace makes you a magnet for success. Expect fresh <u>new</u> doors of opportunity to open!

— Day Eleven —
MASTER YOURSELF

Bible Verse:
He that hath no rule over his own spirit is like a city that is broken down, and without walls.
Proverbs 25:28

Self-discipline is unifying the body and mind towards a specific goal or purpose. On your road to victory, your first objective is to conquer yourself. Whether you desire to have a sculpted body, start a ministry, play professional sports, move up the corporate ladder, or become a millionaire, self-discipline is an essential ingredient to all success. Nothing of great achievement can be achieved without it.

What you do consistently, you will eventually become. Your habits, rituals, and routines must be congruent with the goals and outcomes you wish to accomplish. One by one, you must overcome the daily temptations that stand against your dreams. Self-discipline is sacrificing the short term benefits for a bigger greater desired outcome. It's a loud declaration to the universe that says what I want to achieve is more important to me than the immediate gratification of the things that prevent me from it.

Champions know that winning is a process. They indoctrinate themselves in a strict regimen that facilitates massive success. In the game of life there's no short cuts or participation trophies. Championships aren't just handed out or inherited, they have to be literally taken with hard work.

Self-mastery cannot be outsourced, it's a choice that only you can make. The price of victory must be paid with sweat day in and day out. Gaining control over one's self is the most challenging of all achievements, but it's also the most rewarding. Success requires restraint, willpower, and total mind control. Bringing yourself under total submission is not easy, but your destiny depends on it.

Greatness is in you, but you must make sacrifices to access it. Devotion is the difference between being mediocre and becoming a legend. For real champions, no excuse is acceptable. If you are of average talent, self-discipline must become your weapon. Determination, dedication, and total commitment are the great equalizers. Your willingness to out work and out grind the competition will make all the difference.

People who have no authority over themselves are unfit for leadership. Success avoids the undisciplined like the plague. If you are serious about being successful in life, start cultivating a lifestyle of structure and self-control now. Stop being a slave to your flesh, stop letting your thoughts get the best of you, and once in for all crown yourself master. Stay focused, tap into your "why", and keep your goals in front of you. It's time for you to arise great warrior and do what it takes to become the person God designed you to be.

Positive Affirmation:

I bring every area of my life into submission. I walk at the highest level of self-discipline, consistently doing what it takes to be successful. Today I make a vow to conquer myself.

Self-Assessment Questions:

Why do I want the things I want in life?

What are the daily habits and rituals needed to achieve my goals?

How can I begin to implement these into my life?

In what areas of my life am I already showing self discipline?

What are some of the daily things that successful people do?

What will it feel like when I achieve my goals?

What will my body look like if I exercise the way I should?

What kind of financial benefits will I enjoy by bringing my spending under control?

How bad do I want to be successful?

Am I willing to commit to a life of greatness?

What one thing can I start on today to cultivate a life style of self-discipline?

How far in life can I really go if I conquer myself?

Who are some of the great legends that best represent hard work and self-discipline?

Today's Prayer:

Father, thank you for giving me the strength to overcome myself. Help me to cultivate a life of structure and self-discipline. Thank you for giving me the power to bring my mind and flesh under total submission in Jesus' name. Amen.

Success Quotes:

In reading the lives of great men, I found that the first victory they won was over themselves... self-discipline with all of them came first.
—Harry S. Truman

Self-discipline begins with the mastery of your thoughts. If you don't control what you think, you can't control what you do. Simply, self-discipline enables you to think first and act afterward.
—Napoleon Hill

Self-discipline is often disguised as short-term pain, which often leads to long-term gains. The mistake many of us make is the need and want for short-term gains (immediate gratification), which often leads to long-term pain.
—Charles F. Glassman

We are what we repeatedly do, excellence then is not an act, but a habit.
—Aristotle

Success is nothing more than a few simple disciplines, practiced every day.
—Jim Rohn

Nothing is more harmful to the service, than the neglect of discipline; for that discipline, more than numbers, gives one army superiority over another.
—George Washington

For a man to conquer himself is the first and noblest of all victories.
—Plato

There is little that can withstand a man who can conquer himself.
—Louis XIV

It was character that got us out of bed, commitment that moved us into action and discipline that enabled us to follow through.
—Zig Ziglar

But I discipline my body and keep it under control, lest after preaching to others I myself should be disqualified.
—1 Corinthians 9:27

If we don't discipline ourselves, the world will do it for us.
—William Feather

Mastering others is strength. Mastering yourself is true power.
—Lao Tzu

Your Action Steps:

1. Let your goals, values, and principles dictate your actions instead of your feelings and emotions. (Detoxing emotionally will increase your self-control.)
2. Ask this question: Is what I'm about to do moving towards my goal or away from it?
3. Make sure you have a strong enough WHY for whatever it is you wish to accomplish. (If you are having trouble staying disciplined, your WHY needs to be re-examined.)
4. Get in motion. (Motion creates energy, momentum, and power.)
5. Set up self-defense systems for the times of day you're most tempted to slip up.

Note: A person who is plugged into their calling, who knows their WHY, and is engaged in doing their passion is less likely to lose focus.

Inspiration For Victory:

Do not be deceived by your current struggles, God has an amazing plan for you!

— Day Twelve —
PLUG INTO THE POWER

Bible Verse:
Love is patient, love is kind. It does not envy, it does not boast, it is not proud. It is not rude, it is not self-seeking, it is not easily angered, it keeps no records of wrongs. Love does not delight in evil but rejoices with the truth. It always protects, always trusts, always hopes, always perserveres.
1 Corinthians 13:4-7

God is love and whatever is not of love is not of God. Love has an eternal infinite vibration that reaches to the core of everything in existence. It is by far the most powerful thing in the universe. All miracles originate from it. All powers of nature bow to it. All success hinges on it.

We overcome not by force, might, or money, nor by our knowledge, talents, or connections. We are victors, not because of what we do, but because God loves us. What Jesus did for us on the cross empowers us by grace to breakthrough all barriers.

You are God's ambassador on earth, with a single agenda, and that's to love. The more fluent you are in this universal language, the greater your circle of influence will be. Love is more than just an emotional feeling, its spiritual ballet. The act and expression of this positive energy creates all the good in the world. You can transform anything in your life by plugging into this frequency.

When you adhere to the law of love, you ascend in consciousness to the maximum level of awareness. Through the eyes of love you will not only be able to see, but to truly understand. Being firmly rooted in its power allows you to approach life from a place of strength. By consistently projecting this divine energy, your options and outcomes become limitless.

Love is a super highway, those that travel on it are destined to impact the world. It is the master key that grants access to the spirit realm of all creation. To love is the highest display of wisdom, the highest form of trust, and the highest form of worship.

Your road to prosperity and abundance passes directly through the gate of serving others.

Building your future on the columns of grace is the only absolute guarantee of success. Channel your affection to the people around you and love your neighbor as you love yourself. Show people you truly care about their wellbeing. Sowing daily seeds of compassion and unselfishness will give you more positive return than any other investment you can make.

Shift from a state of needing love to one of bleeding love. Never enter a room without it, never go a day without giving it. Release this catalyst of change into every environment you infiltrate. Instead of wishing for a miracle, become the miracle. Incorporating the gift of love into every aspect of your life will make you a real difference maker.

Positive Affirmation:

I love God with all my heart, mind, and soul and I love my neighbor as I love myself. Unconditionally I give, peacefully I live, for day by day I walk in grace.

Self-Assessment Questions:

Who do I love the most?
How does it feel inside to love unrestrained?
What does it feel like to love my neighbor as I love myself?
How can I express my love at a higher level?
What is the body language of a person who truly loves others?
How can I apply divine love to every area of my life?
What do I love most about myself?
How can I give away more love without needing in return?
At what moment in my life did I feel most loved?
How can I express my love without using words to do it?
Who do I know that best represents unconditional love?
When did I most express unselfishness to someone else?
What kind of a mindset does love derive from?
What two commandments did Jesus say summed up the whole law?

Today's Prayer:
Lord, I pray for you to help me love others unconditionally. Show me how to put your grace into action. Empower me to radiate with your kindness in Jesus' name. Amen.

Success Quotes:

Darkness cannot drive out darkness: only light can do that. Hate cannot drive out hate: only love can do that.
—Martin Luther King Jr.

Love is like the wind, you can't see it but you can feel it.
—Nicholas Sparks

Loving others always costs us something and requires effort. And you have to decide to do it on purpose. You can't wait for a feeling to motivate you.
—Joyce Meyer

When I despair, I remember that all through history the way of truth and love have always won. There have been tyrants and murderers, and for a time, they can seem invincible, but in the end, they always fall. Think of it--always.
—Mahatma Gandhi

We loved with a love that was more than love.
—Edgar Allan Poe

Three things will last forever- faith, hope, & love; & the greatest of these is love.
—1 Corinthians 13:13

Love is not affectionate feeling, but a steady wish for the loved person's ultimate good as far as it can be obtained.
—C.S. Lewis

When you receive God's love and encouragement, it will empower you to do more than you ever thought possible.
—Victoria Osteen

One word Frees us of all the weight and pain of life:
That word is love.
—Sophocles

To love oneself is the beginning of a lifelong romance.
—Oscar Wilde

It is good to love many things, for therein lies the true strength, and whosoever loves much performs much, and can accomplish much, and what is done in love is well done.
—Vincent van Gogh

In the harshest place on Earth, love finds a way.
—Morgan Freeman

Love has nothing to do with what you are expecting to get - only with what you are expecting to give - which is everything.
—Katharine Hepburn

Love is an element which though physically unseen is as real as air or water. It is an acting, living, moving force... it moves in waves and currents like those of the ocean.
—Prentice Mulford

Love is metaphysical gravity.
—R. Buckminster Fuller

The greatest science in the world; in heaven and on earth; is love.
—Mother Teresa

When we love, we always strive to become better than we are. When we strive to become
better than we are, everything around us becomes better too.
—Paulo Coelho

The key to winning is choosing to do God's will and loving others with all you've got.
—Lou Holtz

A loving heart is the beginning of all knowledge.
—Thomas Carlyle

Of all the things Christ wants for us, loving Him and focusing our attention on Him are the most important.
—Charles Stanley

God proved His love on the Cross. When Christ hung, and bled, and died, it was God saying to the world, "I love you."
—Billy Graham

To love another person is to see the face of God.
—Victor Hugo

You can see God from anywhere if your mind is set to love and obey Him.
—Aiden Wilson Tozer

Suffering passes, while love is eternal. That's a gift that you have received from God. Don't waste it.
—Laura Ingalls Wilder

Your Action Steps:

1. Express God's love to a stranger by giving them a nice compliment and a warm caring smile. (Start a Smile ministry.)
2. Offer encouraging words to those around you going through difficulties.
3. Volunteer to help feed the homeless.
4. When going through the drive through, pay for the person's meal in the car behind you.
5. Call every one of your friends and family and tell them how much you love them.
6. Do something kind anonymously for your next-door neighbors.
7. Spend time spreading love and joy at your local nursing home.
8. Become a big brother or sister to an orphan.
9. When you go to a restaurant, regardless of the service, leave your server or waiter a really big tip and sign the bill with a really kind note to express your appreciation.
10. Go to your local hospital and pray with the people who have friends or family members in critical condition.
11. Help raise money for someone who just lost their job.
12. Find someone who needs a big hug and give it to them.

Note: The things on this list are just some examples to help get you started. Find a way today to express God's love to others and Jesus will take care of the rest!

Inspiration For Victory:

God always blesses and honors those who display his love to others.

— Day Thirteen —
STAY IN YOUR LANE

Bible Verse:
I will give thanks to You, for I am fearfully and wonderfully made; Wonderful are Your works, And my soul knows it very well.
Psalms 139:14

You are an original and there's no one else like you in the world. Champions live every day in the boldness of being themselves. You were never meant to be a carbon copy of anyone, God strategically designed you for greatness. Life is your canvass, grab the paint brush and express yourself. When you can show the world who you really are, without any reluctance, without any fear, and without needing people to accept you, only then can you truly be the artist you were created to be.

All that you want, crave, and desire inside can be found in your own uniqueness. Stop chasing other people's dreams. Stop running from yourself. Quit being the person other people want you to be and start living the life God planned for you. It's impossible to consistently do the things it takes to become successful, when you are not being true to who you really are. To fully walk through the door of victory, you must be in your assigned calling. When you stay in your own lane and build around the strengths God gave you, you will begin to attract success.

Drown out the worldly expectations of what you should be and just be who you are. Listen to your own intuition, the whispering spirit that will guide you to your destiny. Stay grounded. Stay connected to the voice on the inside of you crying out to reveal itself to the world. You already know inside who you are supposed to be, so stop searching. When you finally submit to your own identity, you will then begin to walk in the blessing.

Refusing to accept the role you have been assigned leads to internal conflict. This misalignment will attract all kinds of strife and

...order into your life. Honesty is the first step to bringing your spirit back into harmony. Being real translates to inner peace and sound mental health. When you are comfortable in your own skin, your relationships with others will really begin to flourish. There's nothing more beautiful, more powerful, and more seductive than a person comfortable in their own skin.

Bonafide success can only be obtained and sustained through genuine expression of the truth. Be aware at all times of the war that rages over your identity. Society will try to conform you, try to break you, and most of all attempt to label you. The battleground is over self and you are under siege. Don't join the army of the clones. Be yourself. Take off the mask and let the world bask in the beauty of an original. Be your own star on the stage of life. Accept inside that you are good enough and worthy enough to be loved for the person you really are.

No one can be a better version of you than you. Success will not make you love yourself, but loving yourself will create the environment needed for you to thrive. Make a vow today to stay in your lane and let the real you break forth into the light.

Positive Affirmation:
I accept who I am and choose to let others see the real me. I embrace my own identity and the freedom that comes with it. I vow today to be an original and to stay true to who I really am.

Self-Assessment Questions:

What does being true to myself mean?

How can I be more authentic expressing who I really am?

How would my life improve if I showed more of the real me?

How long can I continue to imitate someone I was never designed to be?

What times in the past did I most show my true colors?

When do I most hide my true identity from others?

How does it feel when I'm just being myself?

Who is the realest person I know?

What about myself do I need to display more of?

Who knows the real me?

In what areas of my life do I most need to express my true self?

What would I gain most by displaying to others who I really am?

Do I dress the way I do because I like it or do I do it because I think that's what the world expects of me?

Why do I feel such a need to have the acceptance of others?

Wouldn't it just be easier for me to be the person God made me to be?

Today's Prayer:
I pray today, Father, for the courage and boldness to display my real identity. Help me to be comfortable in my own skin. Lead me away from anything that is not aligned with the original version you made of me in Jesus' name. Amen.

Success Quotes:

Be who you are and say what you feel, because those who mind don't matter, and those who matter don't mind.
—Bernard M. Baruch

To be yourself in a world that is constantly trying to make you something else is the greatest accomplishment.
—Ralph Waldo Emerson

Always be a first rate version of yourself and not a second rate version of someone else.
—Judy Garland

When you are content to be simply yourself and don't compare or compete, everyone will respect you.
—Lao Tzu

Be yourself- not your idea of what you think somebody else's idea of yourself should be.
—Henry David Thoreau

Don't compromise yourself - you're all you have.
—John Grisham

We must not allow other people's limited perceptions to define us.
—Virginia Satir

Always be yourself, express yourself, have faith in yourself, do not go out and look for a successfull personality and duplicate it.
—Bruce Lee

Wake-up! Think for yourself, be yourself and return to what is real.
—Bryant McGill

Don't dilute yourself for any person or any reason. You are enough! Be unapologetically you.
—Steve Maraboli

I think of life itself now as a wonderful play that I've written for myself, and so my purpose is to have the utmost fun playing my part.
—Shirley MacLaine

Imitation is suicide.
—Ralph Waldo Emerson

Your Action Steps:
1. Acknowledge and accept the person God designed you to be.
2. Write down a list of the times in your life when you felt most authentic.
3. Examine what you were thinking or doing at the time that made you feel that way.
4. Write down a list of your personal strengths.
5. Write down a list of ways that you can build more of your life around your answers for Questions 3 & 4.
6. Examine your dreams and goals to make sure that they are really yours and not just borrowed from someone you admire.
7. Audit your dress code to see if what you are wearing every day is align with who you really are.

Inspiration For Victory:
When you are being who God designed you to be, you are blessed and unstoppable!

— Day Fourteen —
GO ALL IN

Bible Verse:
Commit thy works unto the LORD, and thy thoughts shall be established.
Proverbs 16:3

Dedication is the bridge that connects dreams to reality. Success is not for the timid, the fearful, or the indecisive. It's reserved for the bold, dedicated, and fearless. Victory is set aside for the passionately persistent, those willing to put it all on the table no matter what the risk.

Commitment is loyalty to a specific desired outcome with consistent action behind it to prove it. It's a state of mind, a way of living, a totally different level of being. Having a backup plan is just evidence that a person doesn't fully believe they can accomplish what they want in life. It's rooted in fear and doubt, the two things that champions must completely eradicate from their lives.

Focus on one outcome and one outcome only, total victory. Cultivate a do or die mentality and let your work ethic be your voice. Perfect your craft. Master your talent. Dedicate yourself with discipline, then go out and conquer the impossible. Put in the work that it takes to reach your goals, so that you can do the mighty things God has laid out for you.

Only when you crawl out to the unknown will you fully be reliant on God, but that's the only place where you are truly invincible. When you walk your faith out with sweat, destiny won't abandon you. You are a warrior and nothing can defeat you. You don't need a safety net when you refuse to be denied. Hour after hour, keep knocking on the door until the hinges fall off. Make practice your art, repetition your addiction. Champions do it right until they forget how to ever do it wrong. Sacrifice the short term gratifications for your place at the table of greatness.

Going all in is your road out of mediocrity. So what if you make some mistakes along the way, just make them at full speed. Learn from them and push on. Use every set back as a set up to launch you to greater heights. Let your actions proclaim your allegiance to success. Declare all-out war on failure. Refuse to settle for average. Staying in the comfort zone is for the masses, not for the blessed and unstoppable. Surround yourself with people who know what real commitment looks like. Every day hold yourself accountable to doing what it takes to reach the top.

All change is rooted in decision. Being a champion is a choice that only you can make. Once you decide to commit to success, you must reinforce this decision every day. Only by going all in with a relentless determination to succeed will you ever transform your dreams into reality.

Positive Affirmation:
I dedicate my life wholeheartedly to achieving my life's goals with extraordinary resolve. I will back up every intention and plan that I have with total commitment. Failure is not an option for me! I am going all in!

Self-Assessment Questions:

What am I going to totally commit my life to?

How does it feel inside to be 100% committed to achieving something?

Who is the most devoted and committed person I know?

What level of focus is it going to take to achieve the goals that I want to obtain?

How far could I really go in life if I went all in?

What does being committed really mean to me?

What one thing can I commit to doing today?

What makes successful people so dedicated?

When in my life have I shown the most resolve to achieve something?

What does the vocabulary of a committed person sound like?

What does a champion's daily schedule look like?

On a scale from one to ten, what's my current level of commitment to accomplishing my dream?

Today's Prayer:

Father, help me to make the decision to totally commit myself to accomplishing the dreams you have put in me. Strengthen my resolve so that I can fully dedicate my life to doing the things it takes to being successful. Help me to rid my mind of any doubt, fear, or hesitation that stands in the way of reaching my goals in Jesus' name. Amen.

Success Quotes:

When you're surrounded by people who share a passionate commitment around a common purpose, anything is possible.
—Howard Schultz

We cannot be sure of having something to live for unless we are willing to die for it.
—Ernesto Guevara

Desire is the key to motivation, but it's determination and commitment to an unrelenting pursuit of your goal - a commitment to excellence – that will enable you to attain the success you seek.
—Mario Andretti

Without commitment, you cannot have depth in anything, whether it's a relationship, a business or a hobby.
—Neil Strauss

There's no scarcity of opportunity to make a living at what you love. There is only a scarcity of resolve to make it happen.
—Wayne W. Dyer

There's a difference between interest and commitment. When you're interested in doing something, you do it only when it's convenient. When you're committed to something, you accept no excuses - only results.
—Kenneth H. Blanchard

Seems to me that there is a fine line between insanity and dedication… I call that line commitment.
—Jeremy Aldana

One person with commitment accomplishes more than a thousand with an opinion.
—Orrin Woodward

Persistence and passion will make you invincible.
—Christian Baloga

If you believe in yourself and have dedication and pride – and never quit, you'll be a winner. The price of victory is high but so are the rewards.
—Coach Paul Bryant

Your Action Steps:
Find a way to dedicate at least an hour more each day to achieving your goals. In a week's time that's seven more hours you applied to doing the things needed to succeed. Anything on your daily schedule that does not move you closer to your dreams <u>must be removed</u>. Commit to allocating every second of down time you have towards laying the foundation for success.

Inspiration For Victory:
You are surrounded by God's favor, step out with boldness and pursue your dreams!

— Day Fifteen —
ASSEMBLE WISE COUNSEL

Bible Verse:
Plans fail for lack of counsel, but with many advisers they succeed.
Proverbs 15:22

One of the most important keys to success is assembling the right team of advisors. Your mentors should have a respected knowledge in their field, a willingness to share information, demonstrate a positive attitude, possess excellent communication skills, and exhibit the highest level of integrity. Success is not a solo act. It requires a balance of backgrounds, wisdom, and experience in many different areas all harmonizing for one specific purpose.

Your mastermind alliance will help you navigate the oceans of life. When storms come, they will guide you away from the rocks and assist you in getting to your desired designation. Mentors can save you years of struggle and heartache. Surrounding yourself with experienced associates gives you access to a rolodex of contacts, knowledge, and expertise that will all be essential to your future.

Stay around positive people who will motivate you, challenge you, but at the same time give it to you straight. Choose consultants of different backgrounds in areas that you might not be well versed in, so that your strengths and weaknesses can be counterbalanced.

Every major corporation has a board of directors guiding their decisions. Applying this powerful process in your own life can be the difference maker. Your mastermind group should hold you accountable to all the principles laid out in this book. They will be able to see what you are doing from a different perspective and shield you from making costly mistakes. You want to assemble a team of experts who have actually achieved the highest levels of success and know what it takes to get there. Congregate around overcomers who have failed hard in life, but turned it around and succeeded big anyway.

Search for problem solvers and gifted associates that can find solutions to whatever circumstance that might arise. Humble yourself before them. Bow at the throne of wise counsel. They have been where you are trying to go, so listen to them with an open mind. Heed to their advice and constructive criticism, then implement the changes exactly the way they tell you to.

Whenever wisdom assembles in unity, there's a synergy of energy created. Momentum begins to churn. Situations and circumstances begin to change. Excitement and motivation increases. Collaborations spawn brainstorming and fresh new ideas that will accelerate you towards your goals. Plugging into the wisdom and experience of your mentors will expose you to new opportunities to learn, grow, and expand. Their feedback is worth its weight in gold. In today's competitive environment, having wise advisors is not an option, it's an absolute necessity. Only by leveraging the wisdom of great minds can you reach the height of your own greatness.

Positive Affirmation:
I surround myself with wise counsel. By listening and heading to their advice, I am more equipped for the life of success that I desire! I feel so grateful for the wise, experienced, and honest people I have around me.

Self-Assessment Questions:

Who are the wisest and smartest people I know?
Who can I surround myself with to give me wise counsel?
In what areas of my life do I need to seek advice?
When in the past have I really benefitted from mentorship?
Who would be some great mentors for me to study under now?
Who has the most integrity that I know?
Who would be willing to hold me accountable to the righteous values that I want to live by?
Who do I know that will be honest with me and give it to me straight?
Why does having a team of great advisors make me stronger?
What are some of the immediate benefits I would experience by assembling a great team of advisors?
What does it feel like to have some amazing people to turn to in difficulty situations?
In what areas of strength can I mentor others?
What's one thing today I can do to begin assembling my mastermind group?

> **Today's Prayer:**
> Thank you, Father, for surrounding me with wise counsel. Give me the strength to humble myself and to follow the advice of the mentors you are sending me. I pray for you to help me assemble people of your righteous character to guide me in every area of my life in Jesus' name. Amen.

Success Quotes:

Where no counsel is, the people fall: but in the multitude of counselors there is safety.
—Proverbs 11:14

Whatever you do in life, surround yourself with smart people who'll argue with you.
—John Wooden

Surround yourself with the best people you can find, delegate authority, and don't interfere as long as the policy you've decided upon is being carried out.
—Ronald Reagan

Many receive advice, only the wise profit from it.
—Publilius Syrus

The best thing to do when you find yourself in a hurting or vulnerable place is to surround yourself with the strongest, finest, most positive people you know.
—Kristin Armstrong

You can't build any kind of organization if you're not going to surround yourself with people who have experience and skill base beyond your own.
—Howard Schultz

A single conversation across the table with a wise man is worth a month's study of books.
—Chinese Proverb

Nothing is impossible for those who act after wise counsel and careful thought.
—Turuvalluvar Quotes from The Kural No. 142

He who can take advice is sometimes superior to him who can give it.
—Karl von Knebel

Surround yourself with people who are smarter than you.
—Russell Simmons

The disciplined Christian will be very careful what sort of counsel he seeks from others. Counsel that contradicts the written Word is ungodly counsel. Blessed is the man that walketh not in that.
—Elisabeth Elliot

A fool despises good counsel, but a wise man takes it to heart.
—Confucius

Your Action Steps:
This week identify the top three people in your field, then reach out to them to see if they would be open to mentoring you. Each week search for more and more ways to connect with smart, talented, and experienced veterans who are already doing what you want to do. You will be surprised at how open some of them will be to helping you! <u>Do whatever it takes to get into an environment of wisdom</u>. When you're in the presence of greatness, become a sponge soaking up as much knowledge and understanding as possible.

Inspiration For Victory:
God is sending all the right people into your life to assist you with fulfilling your divine destiny!

— Day Sixteen —
UNIFY YOUR FOCUS

Bible Verse:
Let thine eyes look right on, and let thine eyelids look straight before thee.
Proverbs 4:25

The number one reason people fail to reach their goals is broken focus. The world is full of time bandits and energy draining distractions that constantly claw at us for attention. We are bombarded daily with the realities of life, many of which we have no control over. To be successful we must to learn to overcome these disturbances and stay laser focused on our destiny.

You focus is the steering wheel that guides your mind and emotions. What you think about daily you will begin to move towards. Eventually, you will give birth to your most dominant thoughts. This is why it's so crucial to stay constantly focused on the things that you want to achieve in life. Never allocate time or attention to something that doesn't belong in your future.

Success requires unifying your thoughts and actions behind a single clearly defined purpose. Super achievers put on blinders, so that all they can see is their desired future. You must consolidate all your focus, energy, and resources to the tasks needed to achieve your dreams. Scattering yourself only makes you weaker and less effective.

Massive goals require massive focus. Highly effective people are masters at removing the clutter from their lives. Their daily action lists consist solely of doing the tasks that produce extraordinary outcomes. This type of strategy implemented consistently yields powerful results.

Studies estimate that it takes 10,000 hours to achieve mastery in a field. It's impossible to allocate that much time to your craft unless you remove all the time killers that wage war on success.

Concentrating on fewer things allows you to do the essential tasks needed to make an impact. Focusing allows you to channel your momentum and apply it to places that will actually make a difference.

Dreams are built one brick at a time. To be super successful, you must prioritize and narrow down your activities. Decide the one thing that matters the most and then dedicate every second of your life to bringing it about.

Positive Affirmation:
I am highly focused and purpose driven. I refuse to get distracted by things that do not move me towards my calling. Daily, I review my goals to ensure I stay on the path to achieving them.

Self-Assessment Questions:

What are the most important things in my life?

Where should I place the majority of my attention?

In what area of my life am I currently most focused?

In what area of my life am I most distracted?

Why do I give so much of my time and energy to things that sabotage my success?

How can I better structure my life to avoid distractions?

What one thing should I dedicate my life towards accomplishing?

What are my most productive activities?

What are my least productive activities?

Do I review my goals every day?

If I spent all my time on perfecting my craft how great could I be?

How do successful people stay so focused?

> **Today's Prayer:**
> I pray, Father, for you to help me to stay focused on the most important things in life. Thank you for assisting me with keeping my eyes on your plan. Continue to guide me with your spirit so that I can be mentally and spiritually united in Jesus' name. Amen.

Success Quotes:

Successful people maintain a positive focus in life no matter what is going on around them. They stay focused on their past successes rather than their past failures, and on the next action steps they need to take to get them closer to the fulfillment of their goals rather than all the other distractions that life presents to them.
—Jack Canfield

What you stay focused on will grow.
—Roy T. Bennett

Ultimately, leadership is not about glorious crowning acts. It's about keeping your team focused on a goal and motivated to do their best to achieve it, especially when the stakes are high and the consequences really matter.
—Chris Hadfield

What I've learned in these 11 years is you just got to stay focused and believe in yourself and trust your own ability and judgment.
—Mark Cuban

When every physical and mental resources is focused, one's power to solve a problem multiplies tremendously.
—Norman Vincent Peale

You must be single-minded. Drive for the one thing on which you have decided.
—General George S. Patton

By staying focused on what I intend to create, by believing that the universe is all-providing, and by knowing that I'm worthy of the unlimited beneficence of the Source of being, I just keep attracting prosperity to me.
—Wayne Dyer

That's been one of my mantras - focus and simplicity. Simple can be harder than complex: You have to work hard to get your thinking clean to make it simple. But it's worth it in the end because once you get there, you can move mountains.
—Steve Jobs

When trouble comes, focus on God's ability to care for you.
—Charles Stanley

Your Actions Steps:

1. Set the tone for the day by reviewing your life goals first thing in the morning.
2. Decide the outcomes that need to be accomplished each day that move you towards them.
3. Rate them in order of impact.
4. Structure your schedule around accomplishing the most important objectives first.
5. Make sure every activity on your agenda is improving your chances at success.
6. Delete ALL time and energy killers that distract you from your destiny.
7. Stay focused during the day as you knock out each task one at a time
8. Review your life goals again right before bedtime.

Inspiration For Victory:

God has designed you to make a massive impact on the world, just keep believing!

— Day Seventeen —
SET MASSIVE GOALS

Bible Verse:
And the LORD answered me: "Write the vision; make it plain on tablets, so he may run who reads it. For still the vision awaits its appointed time; it hastens to the end—it will not lie. If it seems slow, wait for it; it will surely come, it will not delay."
Habbakkuk 2:2-3

People who set massive goals accomplish and achieve significantly above and beyond those who do not have them. Having clear laid out objectives for each area of your life will give you a clear sense of purpose. Writing your goals down on paper will help define and clarify what success really means to you. It initiates the transitioning process of pulling dreams out of the thought realm to catapult them into reality.

Only by knowing precisely where you want to go can you plan out an effective strategy to get there. Mapping out short term, mid-term, and long term benchmarks will create order in your life and make you way more productive. Clarifying the specific outcomes you desire will help prevent you from getting distracted and pulled off in a thousand different directions.

Laying out goals the SMART way will help you identify the milestones needed to keep you on a trajectory towards success. SMART goals are Specific, Measurable, Audacious, Relevant, and Time-based. Structuring your dreams, goals, and ambitions this way drastically improves your chances of actually bringing them about.

The first step is to decide what you want to accomplish in each area of your life. The second step is to make each target something measurable. For example, instead of just writing down "I want to be rich", you would quantify it by laying out a more definitive goal of making a million dollars.

Third, make sure what you are aiming for is audacious and exciting. Start right where you are and progressively move towards greater and greater outcomes. Using the previous example of a million dollars, that would be your long term goal, while making an extra hundred dollars a week might be your short term aspiration. The fourth step is to make it relevant towards your own skills, within your knowledge, and something that you have some type of control over. The final step is making it time-based. The key here is to set a time frame that stretches and pushes you to the limit, but at the same time is realistic.

Once you have your goals clearly written out, put them in a place that you can review them daily. Make sure you hold yourself accountable to doing the actions required to reach them. Keep your targets in front of you at all times. Doing this will keep you laser focused and moving towards your dreams.

> **Positive Affirmation:**
> I am crystal clear about what I want in every area of my life. Every day I move closer to my dreams, goals, and ambitions. My daily routine is effectively set up for me to achieve what I have set out to accomplish.

Self-Assessment Questions:

Am I clear about what I want to accomplish in each area of my life?
Have I written my goals down on paper?
What is my timeline for accomplishing them?
Do these targets really stretch me to become the best I can be?
Do these outcomes really excite me?
In what areas can I set my objectives even higher?
Have I placed my goals in a place where I can view them every day?
Are my goals properly structured into short term, mid-term, and long term objectives?
What am I going to do today to start working towards my dreams?
Who do I know that has a clearly written out defined list of goals for their life?
What are my strategies for reaching these awesome ambitions I have?
Am I setting aside time each day to mentally envision myself accomplish my goals?

Today's Prayer:

Thank you, Father, for giving me complete clarity over my life. Help me to stay focused on the goals and dreams you have planted inside me. Assist me in developing the right plans and strategies needed to accomplish them in Jesus' name. Amen.

Success Quotes:

The greater danger for most of us isn't that our aim is too high and miss it, but that it is too low and we reach it.
—Michelangelo

Give me a stock clerk with a goal and I'll give you a man who will make history. Give me a man with no goals and I'll give you a stock clerk.
—J.C. Penney

Our goals can only be reached through a vehicle of a plan, in which we must fervently believe, and upon which we must vigorously act. There is no other route to success.
—Pablo Picasso

Obstacles are things a person sees when he takes his eyes off his goal.
—E. Joseph Cossman

To dream by night is to escape your life. To dream by day is to make it happen.
—Stephen Richards

Set a goal to achieve something that is so big, so exhilarating that it excites you and scares you at the same time.
—Bob Proctor

First reach your target in your mind, then reaching your target in reality will just be a formality!
—Mehmet Murat Ildan

For every God-given goal, He gives grace to accomplish it.
—Lailah Gifty Akita

What you get by achieving your goals is not as important as what you become by achieving your goals.
—Zig Ziglar

Setting goals is the first step in turning the invisible into the visible.
—Tony Robbins

Your Actions Steps:

1. Decide what you want to accomplish in each area of your life and then write it down.
2. Make sure that your outcomes are clearly defined and measurable.
3. Ask yourself this question: Are my goals big enough to stretch me and make me better?
4. Verify that these goals are within your control.
5. Set aggressive but realistic time limits to reach each one of your goals.
6. Keep your goals in front of you so you know what you are working towards every day.

Note: This process should be used for all time frames. (Start with your long term goals and work your way backwards to mid-term/short term) Your short term objectives should move you towards your mid-term goals and your mid-term objectives should move you towards your long term goals etc.

Inspiration For Victory:

Do not be intimidated by the lies of the world, God's explosive favor will thrust you to victory!

— Day Eighteen —
DESTROY THE ENEMY WITHIN

Bible Verse:
Now the works of the flesh are evident: sexual immorality, impurity, sensuality, idolatry, sorcery, enmity, strife, jealousy, fits of anger, rivalries, dissensions, divisions, envy, drunkenness, orgies, and things like these. I warn you, as I warned you before, that those who do such things will not inherit the kingdom of God.
Galatians 5:19-21

Each and everyone of us has a Trojan horse full of inner enemies that if not addressed will limit our success. These seven deadly vices are **Lust**, **Gluttony**, **Greed**, **Sloth**, **Wrath**, **Envy**, and **Pride**. Any one of these self destructive forces can derail your dreams.

To conquer **Lust** you must guard your eyes at all times. Refuse to embrace anything that is not wholesome and pure. Keep your mind and eyes on the things above.

To defeat **Gluttony** you must gain self-discipline over your eating. Incorporating the biblical laws of fasting will give you control over your inner cravings. Adhere to a strict regiment of exercise so that you can have the health and energy required to achieve your goals.

To destroy **Greed** you must apply the weapon of charity. Tithing will grant you the power over money and material possesions. Be generous by giving consistently to the poor and needy.

To annihilate **Sloth** you must be diligent, incorporate effective time management, and push yourself to become all you can be. There is a time for rest, but all laziness must be eradicated.

To overcome **Wrath** you must learn to be patient, empathetic, and more conisderate of those around you. Seeking first to understand others allows you to respond more effectively to each situation.

To master **Envy** you must cultivate a spirit of gratitude. Give thanks at all times for the abundant blessings in your life. Refuse to allow jealousy a foothold in your mind.

To eradicate **Pride** you must stay humble. Find ways to serve and impact those around you. Praying for the success and well being of others will keep your spirit in balance.

By meditating daily on the word of God, you will be able to recognize, expose, and uproot these corruptable forces before they can do damage to your future. Everyday, do an inner scan on your mind and emotions to ensure that these seven vices haven't crawled back into your life. When you fully destroy the enemy within all the external enemies will become irrellevant.

Positive Affirmation:

Today I will be more aware of my thoughts and inner emotions. Whenever my focus shifts away from the spirit of love, I will steer my mind back towards the word of God. I will destroy every foothold the enemy attempts to plant in me with unfaliable scripture.

Self-Assessment Questions:

Which of these seven vices do I battle with most?

How can I improve in this area?

Where is my focus during the times I seem to struggle?

Why is it important for me to overcome this inner challenge?

Who can I trust to hold me accountable for my actions in this area?

What does God's word say about each of these vices?

What are some scriptures I can use to triumph over these challenges?

How has my life been negatively affected by these seven vices?

What are some of the positive victories I've had overcoming them in the past?

Who bests represents strength in the area that I am having the most difficulty with?

How do they handle and respond differently than I do?

What techniques could I use in the heat of the moment to help me act more constructively?

Today's Prayer:

Father, I pray for your strength to overcome all devices of the enemy. Give me a heightened since of awareness so that I can conquer any inner roadblock that might arise. Help me to improve every day so that I can take back full control over my mind and emotions in Jesus' name. Amen.

Success Quotes:

Revenge, lust, ambition, pride, and self-will are too often exalted as the gods of man's idolatry; while holiness, peace, contentment, and humility are viewed as unworthy of a serious thought.
—Charles Spurgeon

Lust is temporary, romance can be nice, but love is the most important thing of all. Because without love, lust and romance will always be short-lived.
—Danielle Steel

He who is not contented with what he has, would not be contented with what he would like to have.
—Socrates

So much attention is paid to the aggressive sins, such as violence and cruelty and greed with all their tragic effects, that too little attention is paid to the passive sins, such as apathy and laziness, which in the long run can have a more devastating effect.
—Eleanor Roosevelt

Greed is a bottomless pit which exhausts the person in an endless effort to satisfy the need without ever reaching satisfaction.
—Erich Fromm

Anger is an acid that can do more harm to the vessel in which it is stored than to anything on which it is poured.
—Mark Twain

The jealous are troublesome to others, but a torment to themselves.
—William Penn

Pride goes before destruction, and a haughty spirit before a fall.
—Proverbs 16:18

One can have no smaller or greater mastery than mastery of oneself.
—Leonardo da Vinci

Your life does not get better by chance. It gets better by change.
—Jim Rohn

> **Your Action Steps:**
> Go to the Victory section in the back of this book. Find the the particular area of your life that you are struggling with most and read the bible verses that address it. Do this every day until the scriptures take firm root in your spirit. Whenever the enemy tries to rear it's ugly head, defend yourself with the unstoppable Word of God. God's grace is sufficient and it will help you overcome any challenge or obstacle that stands in your way!

> **Inspiration For Victory:**
> **God's anointing breaks the yoke and chains of all limitations. Nothing can stand in the way of your dreams!**

— Day Nineteen —
LEVERAGE EVERY SECOND OF YOUR TIME

Bible Verse:
Therefore be careful how you walk, not as unwise men, but as wise, making the most of your time, because the days are evil.
Ephesians 5:15-16

God has given each and every one of us full equality. We all have the same 24 hours in a day to allocate as we see fit. That totals out to 1,440 minutes, or to break it down even smaller to 86,400 seconds. It is extremely important for you to harness each and every one of those seconds and hold them accountable to your success. Those that cannot manage their time are incapable of managing anything else.

Each level up the success ladder you climb requires more and more efficient use of time. The masses structure their days around hours, but super achievers break their day down into 15 minute blocks. "Time Jedis" as I call them, only schedule tasks that move them towards their goals and ignore the rest. They schedule their top priorities first, then anchor the day, week, and month around them.

Successful time management consists of adding activities that are super productive and removing all the time wasters that aren't generating results. To-do lists often just make people busy and divert them from their ultimate objectives. To become more effective, you must allocate your most precious resource towards the things that really matter. When you have a written out plan for the day, your actions will be intentional and strategic, making you less likely to be held hostage by the moment. Things will arise that you did not expect, but having a solid time structure in place will help you navigate the situations more effectively.

Part of time mastery is learning the art of saying no. Don't schedule a meeting to just have a meeting. Make sure there's a solid purpose behind it and only set aside the time need to achieve that. Ultra-productive people understand the 80/20 rule that states you will get 80% of your results from 20% of your activities. Find out what produces your desired results and build your life around it. Successful people don't just manage time, they multiply it by delegating to qualified people. This allows them to stay focused on the activities that drive results.

Each night, plan out the next day. When you wake up you in the morning, make sure you have a set agenda in place. Every second of every minute should be thrusting you in some way towards reaching your targets. Create daily routines that allow you to leverage and maximize your time. Structure the most important things around the times of day when you have the most energy. Whether you use some kind of digital device, online calendar, or just a simple notebook to plan your day, make sure that it is well written out, focused, and structured for success.

Positive Affirmation:

I am a Time Jedi who masters every second of the day. By planning and proper scheduling, I own my day it does not own me. I focus on the top results desired and make sure every one of my actions are effective at bringing them about.

Self-Assessment Questions:

What does a successful person's schedule look like?

How can I structure my daily routine to be more effective at achieving my goals?

What does it feel like to gain back control over my day?

Am I making sure my daily activities align with doing the tasks required to achieving my goals?

In what area do I most need to adjust my time allocation to bring my life into balance?

Am I allocating enough time to my friends and family?

What tasks bring me the most positive results?

How can I structure my week around doing more of these effective activities?

Am I just being busy or am I being effective?

What are the biggest time killers in my life right now?

Do I have a clear vision in my mind for how my day should look?

Who's the most productive time manager I know?

Today's Prayer:

Thank you, Father, for showing me how precious my time is. Help me to allocate this gift you have given me more effectively in every area of my life. Strengthen my wisdom so that I can see ahead of time the things that need to be planned into my schedule. Thank you for assisting me in getting the most out of each and every day in Jesus' name. Amen.

Success Quotes:

Time is the most valuable coin in your life. You and you alone will determine how that coin will be spent. Be careful that you do not let other people spend it for you.
—Carl Sandburg

The bad news is time flies. The good news is you're the pilot.
—Michael Altshuler

Getting things done is not always about managing time; It is about finding that magical time of the day when you work at your best level.
—Vivek Naik

We don't manage time, we manage activities within time.
—Bernard Kelvin Clive

The best time management tool is a clearly defined and definite purpose for your life.
—Tom Cunningham

A man must be master of his hours and days, not their servant.
—William Frederick Book

Time is the only commodity that is irreplaceable: invest it, share it, spend it...but never waste it.
—Tracy Sherwood

The key is in not spending time, but in investing it.
—Stephen R. Covey

Take care of the minutes and the hours will take care of themselves.
—Lord Chesterfield

You cannot kill time without injuring eternity.
—Henry David Thoreau

Time is really the only capital that any human being has, and the only thing he can't afford to lose.
—Thomas Edison

In truth, people can generally make time for what they choose to do; it is not really the time but the will that is lacking.
—Sir John Lubbock

Your Action Steps:
1. Every Sunday write out the most important outcomes to accomplish for the week.
2. Divide each day's schedule into 15 minute blocks.
3. Before you schedule a task on your list always ask yourself this question: Is this activity moving me closer to my goals?
4. Schedule the activities needed to achieve your outcomes around peak energy times when you are most productive.
5. Break big tasks down into smaller chunks to make them more manageable.
6. Explore ways to leverage more of your time by delegating to qualified people.
7. Set designated times to check and respond to emails.

Inspiration For Victory:
Say goodbye to lack and scarcity, the Lord's abundant blessings are about to overtake you!

— Day Twenty —
DECLARE THE BLESSING

Bible Verse:
Death and life are in the power of the tongue: and they that love it shall eat the fruit thereof.
Proverbs 18:21

God has given each of us the power to create with our mouths. The words we speak sow the seeds of our future. Speaking declarations that align with God's word bring our mind, body, and spirit into agreement. If we want to walk in the fullness of his blessing, we must constantly confess words full of life and victory.

What we verbalize is a direct reflection of the beliefs we have internalized. The way we choose to express ourselves verbally dictates what we attract into our lives. We have the ability to bless, curse, heal, or destroy every time we utter something out of our mouths. Acknowledging this transformative power is essential to building a life of success.

Words set outcomes into motion, therefore it's vital for us to think before we speak. We must stay disciplined keeping watch over our mouth at all times. When we learn to tame our tongue, we take control of our destiny.

The ancient kings never spoke like peasants, therefore they became kings. Sitting on their thrones they didn't wish and hope for things to happen, they boldly decreed them. The old royalty were fully aware of the authority their words had. By faith, we too are of the royal ruling bloodline. Our mouths carry full command of the realm, influencing every aspect of our lives.

Success has to be first spoken into existence. Each word we speak is either carrying us closer or further away from our dreams. Whether we are encouraging a friend, launching a new business, or leading an organization, every verbal expression sends out a wave of energy impacting the environment around us. The things we say, when applied with the other natural laws in this book, have the power to change the world.

During serious times of trouble your mouth is your most effective weapon. No matter what challenges you are facing, keep declaring positive confessions over your life. One day you will reap what you have sown, so make sure you are planting the type of seeds you want to see grow in your future.

> **Positive Affirmation:**
> I choose today to speak powerful words of life. No corrupt communication shall proceed out of my mouth. I boldly declare the positive things I desire to happen with absolute faith and authority. I exhale encouraging words of inspiration into the lives of those around me.

Self-Assessment Questions:

Are the words I'm speaking throughout the day filled with faith, hope, and love?
Is my daily vocabulary aligned with the word of God?
In what area of my life do I need to speak more positive?
Does speaking negative about myself or others help bring my dreams alive?
How would using a better choice of words help my relationships?
In what ways do I verbally articulate my love for friends and family?

Am I declaring daily blessings of health and prosperity over them?
How do I feel when I express words of encouragement to others?
What does the language of champions sound like?
Do I consider the power behind my words before verbalizing them?
Do I regularly declare my positive affirmations out loud?
What kind of conversations do I normally take part in?
If someone over heard me talking would they know that I am a child of God?

Today's Prayer:
Thank you, Father, for helping me to understand the true power of the spoken word. Grant me divine awareness today so that I can speak your blessings over the people and things around me in Jesus' name. Amen

Success Quotes:

But if thought corrupts language, language can also corrupt thought.
—George Orwell

Words are spiritual. Think, speak and affirm positive words.
—Lailah Gifty Akita

The words that come out of our mouth go into our own ears as well as other people's, and then they drop down into our soul where they give us either joy or sadness, peace or upset, depending on the types

of words we have spoken.
—Joyce Meyer

The limits of my language means the limits of my world.
—Ludwig Wittgenstein

But the human tongue is a beast that few can master. It strains constantly to break out of its cage, and if it is not tamed, it will turn wild and cause you grief.
—Robert Greene

Remember not only to say the right thing in the right place, but far more difficult still, to leave unsaid the wrong thing at the tempting moment.
—Benjamin Franklin

Words are singularly the most powerful force available to humanity. We can choose to use this force constructively with words of encouragement, or destructively using words of despair. Words have energy and power with the ability to help, to heal, to hinder, to hurt, to harm, to humiliate and to humble.
—Yehuda Berg

So shall my word be that goeth forth out of my mouth: it shall not return unto me void, but it shall accomplish that which I please, and it shall prosper in the thing whereto I sent it.
—Isaiah 55:11

Think twice before you speak, because your words and influence will plant the seed of either success or failure in the mind of another.
—Napoleon Hill

When you realize the awesome power of words, you can change lives.
—Tammy Kling

> **Your Action Steps:**
> First thing every morning when you wake up, start declaring God's blessings and favor over your life. Pronounce and affirm the positive things you wish to give birth to in your life with energy and expectation. Remember that the words you speak are seeds of power that set in motion the destiny you will inherit. Guard your mouth throughout the day to make sure nothing you say contradicts your amazing future!

> **Inspiration For Victory:**
> # The obstacles you are facing might seem insurmountable, but <u>God still moves</u> mountains!

— Day Twenty-One —
LET YOUR GRIND DO ALL THE TALKING

Bible Verse:
A slack hand causes poverty, but the hand of the diligent makes rich.
Proverbs 10:4

Your mind imagines the dream, but in order for destiny to bloom it must be constantly watered with blood, sweat, and tears. Success comes directly off the assembly line of an intense work ethic. Minimum effort is not an option for someone who wants to live at the highest level of existence. Champions can't take days off. There's so much competition in the world for such a small space of success, if you don't go all out every day, you're never going to make it.

Hard work is the membership fee that filters out the weak from the strong. The respect and credibility required for high achievement is so pricey that only the rich in struggle can afford it. Winners only have one goal they aspire to and that's greatness. They bang, hammer, and chisel on their craft with maximum effort until success becomes their David. Applying this type of relentless pressure allows them to overcome any talent deficiencies they might have.

Legends refuse to give anything less than 120%, because that's the only level of effort they know. Mediocre is a word in a foreign language that they don't comprehend. Good is not good enough, because they recognize the greatness of the creator in them. They hold themselves to the highest standard, for the mere fact that they are not just doing it for themselves, they are doing it to honor the God they serve. Passion mixed with years of perspiration grants them worldwide access. Grind and hustle are universal words respected and admired in every culture. Their work ethic will carry them to places 99% of the world will never see.

Find out the most important factors that determine success in your field and then put all your time, energy, and focus on them. Grinding all day doing the wrong things will not get you where you want to go. You must out work your competitors in the areas that actually decide victory. Put your 120% towards the things that really matter and stay there.

Many people can give their best for three or four days maybe even a week or two, but not many can sustain it for three years, five years, or a decade. Things worth achieving don't come overnight, it takes years of gestation and preparation to bring a dream into existence. A successful business plan isn't built around wishing, hoping, or sheer luck… it's laid on a solid structure of discipline, commitment, and fanatical labor.

The world belongs to the ones who purchase it in sweat. What you accomplish in life will be equivalent to the sum level of the effort you exerted. There's no goal or ambition that can deny the person who masters the art of hard work. Success doesn't have to be complex, just decide what you want and then grind at the level it takes to get it.

Positive Affirmation:

My grind and effective work ethic will become my weapon. From this day forward, no one in my field will ever outwork me again! My hard work and sweat will water my dreams. I will give 120% day in and day for as long as it takes to accomplish my goals!

Self-Assessment Questions:

What level of effort have I been applying towards reaching my goals?

How can I increase my work ethic to a level that will insure success?

Who's working the hardest in my field or profession?

How many hours do I need to grind each day to achieve greatness?

How can I work smarter and more effectively?

Am I willing to pay the price for the things I want in life?

When in the past did my hard work payoff?

What does it feel like when I give my all to something?

Who best exemplifies hard work and heroic effort?

Am I willing to keep up the intensity day in and day out needed to be successful?

In the past, what has kept me from giving my all?

Do blood, sweat, and tears intimidate me?

How many more days of my life can I waste by putting in minimum effort?

Today's Prayer:

I pray today, Father, that you would instill in me the work ethic required to be successful in life. Increase my endurance, my stamina, and my energy so that I can allocate my all to accomplishing the goals and dreams you put inside me in Jesus' name. Amen.

Success Quotes:

If people knew how hard I had to work to gain my mastery, it would not seem so wonderful at all.
—Michelangelo

Great or average? If you want to become great, you have to pay the price…a price the average are unwilling to pay.
—Eric Thomas

I've viewed myself as slightly above average in talent. And where I excel is ridiculous, sickening work ethic.
—Will Smith

People don't understand that when I grew up, I was never the most talented. I was never the biggest. I was never the fastest. I certainly was never the strongest. The only thing I had was my work ethic, and that's been what has gotten me this far.
—Tiger Woods

The fight is won or lost far away from witnesses – behind the lines, in the gym, and out there on the road, long before I dance under those lights.
—Muhammad Ali

A man must drive his energy, not be driven by it.
—William Frederick Book

In fact, researchers have settled on what they believe is the magic number for true expertise: ten thousand hours.
—Malcolm Gladwell

The dictionary is the only place that success comes before work. Work is the key to success, and hard work can help you accomplish anything.
—Vince Lombardi

No matter how you are feeling, get up every morning and prepare to let your light shine forth.
—Paulo Coelho

Your Actions Steps:
1. Decide whether or not your dream is worth the time, energy, and effort required to make it a reality. If it is, then make a commitment to yourself right now to give 120% effort every single day from here forward to making it happen. (If it's not, then dream one that is worthy of giving your all to.)
2. Set the tone for the day by establishing a morning routine of power and purpose.
(The key here is to take ownership of the day by getting in motion.)
3. Stay charged up by eating healthy and exercising regularly.
4. Remove and eliminate ALL distractions from your life.
5. Figure out the amount of hours required each day to achieve greatness in your field and then structure your schedule around that.
6. Every time someone doubts or criticizes you, respond by increasing the level of hours you are putting in towards your dream. (Use it for fuel and go harder!)
7. Stop making excuses, and just go do what it takes to get the things you want in life!

Inspiration For Victory:
God is blessing you with energy and a supernatural work ethic that will make you a thousand times more!

— Day Twenty-Two —
CHASE WISDOM

Bible Verse:
Blessed are those who find wisdom, those who gain understanding, for she is more profitable than silver and yields better returns than gold.
Proverbs 3:13-14

Solomon, the wisest and richest man to ever live, said "Wisdom is the principal thing; therefore get wisdom: and with all thy getting get understanding" (Proverbs 4:7). God put in place universal laws and principles that if tapped into properly will produce success. In order for us to walk in the fullness of the blessing, we must aquire the knowledge and information needed to succeed and then effectively apply it.

Wisdom is a three step process:
Step One: Aquire accurate knowledge.
Step Two: Gain full revelation and understanding of the knowledge acquired.
Step Three: Properly implement and apply what you have learned to your own life.

The quest for knowledge is a life long journey. To attain wisdom one must be humble, open minded, and, most of all, teachable. Each day we should strive to get better and more equipped for life than the day before. We can achieve this by committing and disciplining ourselves every day to studying the word of God.

Wisdom is accurate knowledge understood and consistently applied. It's a universal master key that will unlock any door you wish it to open. By meditating on the scriptures, we gain divine revelation of the way the world works and how God wants us to carry ourselves. The bible is the greatest book of knowledge ever assembled. It's the official guide to prosperity, happiness, and victory. Build your life around it and success will follow you wherever you go.

The old saying that leaders are readers has never been more accurate than in today's disruptive world. Those that fail to consistently upgrade their knowledge and skill will eventually become obsolete. No matter what field your in, your P.H.D. needs to be in success. Studying the lives of great men and women gives you direct insight into their mindset, principles, and rituals. The more you analyze their daily habits, routines, and processes the more you will uncover their secrets to achievement.

Studies show that millioniares read on average two books per month. The important fact here is not just that they read consistently, it's that they are immersing their minds with a type of knowledge and material that allows them to improve themselves. To become a champion you must master the art of observing, dissecting, and analyzing greatness. Whether it's from the bible, self-help books, videos, or seminars, etc. learn quickly to spot the patterns and strategies being applied that determine success, then seek ways to implement them. Incorporating the wisdom you have learned from the greats into your own life will help you replicate their results and thrust you to the next level.

Positive Affirmation:

Every day is a new opportunity for me to educate and improve myself. I am a sponge constantly studying the lives of great men and women soaking up their wisdom. The more I apply what I have learned the more awesome my life becomes!

Self-Assessment Questions:

In what areas of my life am I lacking knowledge?

What books do I need to be reading?

How much of my time am I allocating for learning and self-improvement each week?

How can I structure my time more effectively so that I can educate myself more?

Who are the experts and masters in my field?

How can I study their work and processes so that I can replicate their successes?

In what other ways besides books can I study the lives of great men and women?

Why is self education so important in today's fast changing world?

What books are champions, millioniares, and other highly successful people reading?

In what ways can I learn to read faster and retain more?

What book have I learned the most from?

What's the difference between knowledge and wisdom?

In what ways can I apply the knowledge I have learned into my life?

Why are the great leaders of the world all avide readers?

What person has taught me the most about life?

> **Today's Prayer:**
> Father, I pray that you increase my wisdom and understanding one hundred fold. Give me the strength and discipline to apply what I have learned more effectively. Help me to stay humble, always seeking to learn and grow in Jesus' name. Amen.

Success Quotes:

Keep this Book of the Law always on your lips; meditate on it day and night, so that you may be careful to do everything written in it. Then you will be prosperous and successful.
—Joshua 1:8

I do not think much of a man who is not wiser today than he was yesterday.
—Abraham Lincoln

By three methods we may learn wisdom: First, by reflection, which is noblest; Second, by imitation, which is easiest; and third by experience, which is the bitterest.
—Confucius

In history, a great volume is unrolled for our instruction, drawing the materials of future wisdom from the past errors and infirmities of mankind.
—Edmund Burke

Prepare for the unknown by studying how others in the past have coped with the unforeseeable and the unpredictable.
—George S. Patton

Any fool can know. The point is to understand.
—Albert Einstein

Yesterday I was clever, so I wanted to change the world. Today I am wise, so I am changing myself.
—Rumi

A wise man will make more opportunities than he finds.
—Francis Bacon

Sometimes it's not enough to know what things mean, sometimes you have to know what things don't mean.
—Bob Dylan

There is a wisdom of the head, and... there is a wisdom of the heart.
—Charles Dickens

Where wisdom reigns, there is no conflict between thinking and feeling.
—C.G. Jung

Employ your time in improving yourself by other men's writings so that you shall come easily by what others have labored hard for.
—Socrates

Your Action Steps:

The greatest success and leadership resource ever written is the book of Proverbs in the Bible. It's conviently divided up into thirty one chapters. Any person who is serious about success should discipline themselves to reading one chapter from it every day. Immersing yourself in the unfaliable wisdom of the wisest and richest King to ever live will truly transform your life!

Inspiration For Victory:

This is the season of preparation. God is equpipping you with everything you need for victory!

— Day Twenty-Three —
CONQUER THE NOW

Bible Verse:
Therefore do not worry about tomorrow, for tomorrow will worry about itself. Each day has enough trouble of its own.
Matthew 6:34

There are three dimensions of time: The past, the present, and the future. The past and future only exist in your mind and have absolutely no power by themselves. The power of Now is all that you have and it's all that truly exists.

Living too much in the past sows the seeds for depression. Living too much in the future causes the mind to manufacture stress and anxiety. Peace only comes from awakening to the "Now". To live in the moment is true enlightenment and the highest level of earthly experience.

Ten percent of your day should consist of planning and envisioning your future, the other ninety percent should be living in the "Now". Your holy spirit, the divine guider, can only be heard in this state. When you embrace the present, the drowning noise of chaos and confusion will dissolve into nothingness. Obstacles that previously existed will crumble right before your eyes.

Faith only exists in the present. You are invincible when you are firmly planted in the moment, for "Now" is where GOD is and always has been. Awakening to this state of consciousness is truly empowering. Don't let the past and future pull your life apart. All your resources and mind power reside in the "Now" and can only be maximized in this state of awareness.

The mind stays in a constant state of motion. To tame it you must get behind the wheel. By being more aware of your thoughts you will be able to recognize exactly what dimension your mind is currently inhabiting. By steering your mental energy back to the

"Now", where it's most effective, you will be fully capable of handling anything that arises. It will allow you to see clearly and to capitalize on all the wonderful opportunities that the Lord has prepared for you.

Being in the "Now" is the most conducive state for healing the body. It allows you to meditate on the word of God in a way that gives divine revelation. Disease can only sustain itself when the mind is in a state of misalignment. Aligning with the present brings the body back into perfect balance. Sickness and disorder cannot continue to exist when you raise the level of your consciousness. The "Now" will starve these weaker states annihilating them completely.

The level of happiness you experience on earth will center around the amount of the "Now" you conquer. Tapping into the power of "Now" will increase your awareness and will allow you to enjoy every ounce of sensation that life has to offer. Allow the past and future to rule their own realms while you dictate and command the current moment. This is where you will feel the most alive, the most joy, and the most loved. The quality of your life will drastically improve when you stay present and cherish the gift of "Now", for without her you do not exist.

Positive Affirmation:
I bring my full attention into the Now. I embrace the powerful sensations of living in this beautiful moment. I lack nothing because everything I need is in the Now.

Self-Assessment Questions:

What does living in the Now mean to me?

What do I place the majority of my focus: past, present, or future?

How can I bring my focus and attention into the present?

How would living in the moment improve my life?

What times can I recall in the past that I lived most in the moment?

How would my health improve if I chose to live in the Now?

What does being present feel like inside?

When I am truly in the moment what sensations are most present in my body?

Who do I know that most represents living in the Now?

When does my mind most wander away from the Now?

How much more peace could I experience by staying in the present?

When stress or anxiety attempt to come on me, where is my focus?

What are some ways to bring my mind and thoughts back into the present?

Today's Prayer:

Father, I pray today for you to make me more aware of when my mind is not fully present. Assist me in steering my thoughts back to the Now so that I can be most productive. Lord help me to surrender the past and future to you so that I can function fully in the gift of the present moment in Jesus' name. Amen.

Success Quotes:

Forever is composed of nows.
—Emily Dickinson

You must live in the present, launch yourself on every wave, find your eternity in each moment. Fools stand on their island of opportunities and look toward another land. There is no other land; there is no other life but this.
—Henry David Thoreau

Happiness, not in another place but this place... not for another hour, but this hour.
—Walt Whitman

Be present in all things and thankful for all things.
—Maya Angelou

Realize deeply that the present moment is all you have. Make the NOW the primary focus of your life.
—Eckhart Tolle

You can take all the pictures you want, but you can never relive the moment the same way.
—Audrey Regan

Wherever you are, be there. If you can be fully present now, you'll know what it means to live.
—Steve Goodier

When you live for every second, tomorrow doesn't matter!
—Stephen Richards

Write it on your heart that every day is the best day in the year.
—Ralph Waldo Emerson

You can clutch the past so tightly to your chest that it leaves your arms too full to embrace the present.
—Jan Glidewell

The ability to be in the present moment is a major component of mental wellness.
—Abraham Maslow

If you are depressed, you are living in the past. If you are anxious, you are living in the future. If you are at peace, you are living in the present.
—Lao Tzu

Your Action Steps:
Start out today by focusing on your breathing. Take a deep breath, hold it for five seconds, and then release it. Do this five times while being completely mindful of every inhale and exhale you make. Heighten your awareness to all the energy your body is radiating. Keep your concentration firmly rooted in the Now. Let all the stress, worries, and fears just melt away. Enjoy and savor every ounce of peace the moment has to offer. Meditating like this for 5-10 minutes will empower you, bring you into balance, and set the tone for the rest of your day

Inspiration For Victory:
God's amazing grace will replenish your strength. Draw your peace and energy from him!

— Day Twenty-Four —
EXERCISE YOUR AUTHORITY

Bible Verse:
But you will receive power when the Holy Spirit comes on you; and you will be my witnesses in Jerusalem, and in all Judea and Samaria, and to the ends of the earth.
Acts 1:8

You have been granted, through grace, the power and authority to accomplish your divine assignment. God has empowered and anointed you to excel. He has placed the seeds of greatness inside of you, and with this anointing all things are possible. Once you become fully awakened to this omnipotent power and where it resides, you will become unstoppable.

God does not want his ambassadors walking around on earth sick, broke, and defeated. There's no glory for him in that. He made you to prosper in every area, so that you can give a shining testimony to the world of his own greatness. Every victory, blessing, and success you experience is designed in some way to put you in position to minister to the lost. He has empowered you to succeed so that you can have greater access to bigger and bigger platforms to pronounce his glory. You are a soldier in the mighty army of God and no great general would send his soldiers out into battle empty handed. He has fully equipped you to be victorious. Your weapons are faith, mind, and the spoken word. These are the most powerful weapons in existence and nothing can stand against them. These are the same weapons Jesus performed all his miracles with and you have complete access to them.

God has granted us, as believers, the spiritual authority and power to command into existence all the finished works of Christ. The enemy's strategy has always been to deceive you into believing that you are at the mercy of your circumstances. This is a lie, you have full dominion over all the devices of the enemy. To fully walk in this state of empowerment you must shift from having faith <u>In</u> God to having the faith <u>OF</u> God. When you transition to this state of mind all the power of heaven is at your disposal (according to your faith be it unto you). Lay hands on the sick with the full belief that God still heals today. Use the anointing to express the abundance of life, the peace of God, and the wholeness of the almighty. Apply it towards things that are positive and of good report that cause no harm to others. Walk it out through peace, love, gentleness, and with self-control. Show them on earth a glimpse of what heaven looks like. Using the anointing this way will draw and attract others to the kingdom.

Believe with full confidence that wherever you go God goes also. If the word of God promises you something, then you can rest assure in full faith that you have it. The power is in you, go now and change the world with it!

Positive Affirmation:

I have the power and authority inside of me to fulfill my God given destiny. My purpose is to use this anointing to bring glory to my heavenly father in every aspect of my life. The more success I experience the more opportunities I will have to testify of his great name.

Self-Assessment Questions:

In what ways can I use my success to bring glory to God?

How can I use this authority entrusted to me to help and bless others?

Are there any limits to God's power?

If God is in me can anything stand against me?

Do I understand that grace is a package deal offering me complete forgiveness of my sins and granting me power to testify of the gospel through miracles and amazing works?

In what ways does being successful in my own life convey the awesomeness of God?

Does God want his people to be healthy, happy, and prosperous?

How does it feel inside to know I have been given the complete gift of authority over evil?

What does being blessed really mean to me?

What kind of success would give me the biggest platform to preach the gospel?

Does God's word say that he has placed in me the power to heal others?

In what ways do I envision myself prospering for the kingdom?

Today's Prayer:

Lord, thank you for granting me the power and authority to overcome any obstacle in my life. Make me a great steward of this power you have bestowed on me through Jesus Christ. Help me to use this authority to glorify your name more and more each day in Jesus' name. Amen.

Success Quotes:

Truly I tell you, whatever you bind on earth will be bound in heaven, and whatever you loose on earth will be loosed in heaven.
—Matthew 18:18

Power resides only where men believe it resides.
—George R.R. Martin

We have within us a power that is greater than anything that we shall ever contact in the outer, a power that can overcome every obstacle in our life and set us safe, satisfied and at peace, healed and prosperous, in a new light, and in a new life. Mind, all mind, is right here. It is God's Mind, God's creative Power, God's creative Life. We have as much of this Power to use in our daily life as we can believe in and embody.
—Ernest Holmes

You have the power to heal your life, and you need to know that. We think so often that we are helpless, but we're not. We always have the power of our minds… Claim and consciously use your power.
—Louise L. Hay

It's our faith that activates the power of God.
—Joel Osteen

Having a positive attitude gives you power. This isn't the same kind of power that dictators and warlords seek after, but rather a spiritual power. It's a power that comes to us from God.
—Lindsey Rietzsch

Very truly I tell you, whoever believes in me will do the works I have been doing, and they will do even greater things than these, because I am going to the Father.
—John 14:12

What you have become, remember to glorify God by the work of your hands through his power that is at work within you.
—Carl Lomer Abia

For God hath not given us the spirit of fear; but of power, and of love, and of a sound mind.
—2 Timothy 1:7

> **Your Action Steps:**
> 1. Fully accept Jesus Christ into your heart.
> 2. Confess all your sins to God.
> 3. Bring every area of your life into alignment with His word.
> 4. Believe you have everything the Bible says you have. (Power and Authority)
> 5. Verify through the word that what you are asking for is in agreement with God's word.
> 6. With praise and thanksgiving make your supplications known to Him.
> 7. Pray in Jesus' name with absolute unwavering faith.
> 8. Trust God to intervene on your behalf and He will!
>
> *Note: Once you fully accept Jesus into your heart, you have on the inside of you the same power Christ and his disciples used to perform their miracles with. The Holy Spirit will use you to do the same wonders or even greater miracles to bring glory to God if you allow it to. Remember this: Your level of faith will determine the level of power you have access to. ("According to your faith will it be done to you." Matthew 9:29)*

> **Inspiration For Victory:**
> # No weapon formed against you will prosper, everywhere you go you will flourish!

— Day Twenty-Five —
BUILD A STRONG INNER CIRCLE

Bible Verse:
He that walketh with wise men shall be wise: but a companion of fools shall be destroyed.
Proverbs 13:20

The level of success that you attain will be directly tied to the quality of people you associate with. Those in your inner circle will have a major impact on the way you think, speak, and act. The friends you choose to surround yourself with will ultimately determine your destiny. God has commanded us to go into all the world and preach the gospel and that means to everybody. However, for those who carry influence in our lives and that we interact with on a regular basis we must be more selective.

Studies have shown that your annual income will be the average of the five people you spend time with the most. The principle behind the Law of Five mandates that sooner or later you become who you hang with. This rule applies to family members just as much as it does your friends. Their religious, political, and social views all become contagious. Their opinions on money, fitness, and relationships will directly influence your thinking, that's why it's so important to examine whether or not your circle of five are in alignment with your goals.

Your top priority should be letting go of relationships that drain your energy. The less time you spend with negative unproductive people the more your life will improve. The more you stay around winners and champions, the more their habits will rub off on you.

Success is a team effort, so you must choose your companions wisely. Stay far away from those with questionable character, for to be unequally yoked is inviting disaster. Partner up with people who have the same goals, drive, and ambitions as you do. Affiliate with people who are prospering in their marriages, finances, and relationships so that you can learn as much as you can from them. Build yourself a support system of friends, coworkers, mentors, and family members that bring the best out of you.

Your criteria for retaining or adding members to your inner circle should be that you get stronger in some type of way because of their presence. Limit the time you give to anyone that doesn't support your dreams. Success is determined not just by those that you associate with, but also those that you don't. Your circle of five will speak volumes about you and your future, so do everything in your power to surround yourself with the right people.

Positive Affirmation:
I choose to associate with people of the highest quality who inspire and encourage me to chase my dreams. From this point forward, the people I allow into my inner circle must in some way improve my chances at success. My circle of five will consist of nothing but winners and champions who exemplify greatness!

Self-Assessment Questions:

Who do I spend most of my time with?

Do the five people I hang out with the most hinder or improve my chances at being successful?

Do they believe in God and exhibit the kind of core values I want to represent?

What are their goals in life?

Do they have the same ambition to succeed as me?

Are they making the kind of money I want to make?

Do they encourage me to chase my dreams?

What kind of books are they reading?

Who do I need to spend less time with?

Who do I need to spend more time around

Who in my family is most supportive of my goals

Which family members discourage me the most?

In what ways can I surround myself with more positive people?

Today's Prayer:

Father, help me to surround myself with people of strong character. Show me who I need to spend less time with and who I should associate with more. Place me around a loyal group of encouraging, loving, and talented friends who will assist me in reaching new heights in Jesus' name. Amen.

Success Quotes:

The next best thing to being wise oneself is to live in a circle of those who are.
—C. S. Lewis

You are the average of the five people you spend the most time with.
—Jim Rohn

There are two questions a man must ask himself: The first is 'Where am I going?' and the second is 'Who will go with me?' If you ever get these questions in the wrong order you are in trouble.
—Sam Keen

Some of your friends will not want you to go on. They will want you to stay where they are. Friends that don't help you climb will want you to crawl. Your friends will stretch your vision or choke your dream. Those that don't increase you will eventually decrease you.
—Colin Powell

We acquire the characteristics of the people we associate with on a steady basis.
—Zig Ziglar

Surround yourself with people who are smarter than you. Pick people who are interested in what you're interested in.
—Russell Simmons

Whatever vocation you decide on, track down the best people in the world at doing it and surround yourself with them.
—Scott Weiss

We gain nothing by being with such as ourselves. We encourage one another in mediocrity. I am always longing to be with men more excellent than myself.
—Charles Lamb

It's better to hang out with people better than you. Pick out associates whose behavior is better than yours, and you'll drift in that direction.
—Warren Buffett

Keep away from people who try to belittle your ambitions. Small people always do that, but the really great make you feel that you, too, can become great.
—Mark Twain

Your Actions Steps:
Evaluate the five people you associate with the most and determine whether they are increasing or diminishing your chances at success. Rank their impact on your life from one to five with one being the most negative and five representing the most positive. Begin immediately to distance yourself from anyone who grades out at 1-2. If they rank as a 3, which is neutral, find a way to improve the dynamic of the relationship or begin to limit the time you spend with them. When the sum total of your team of five finally grades out at 20 or better, you've built a strong inner circle of positive and trust worthy people you can achieve success with.

Inspiration For Victory:
Be encouraged, for God will grant you extreme favor with the people needed to help you achieve your dreams!

— Day Twenty-Six —
REFUSE TO CONCEDE

Bible verse of the day:
And let us not grow weary of doing good, for in due season we will reap, if we do not give up.
Galatians 6:9

The secret to success is refusing to give up. Perseverance transforms average everyday people into world champions. No matter what your goals are in life there's going to be massive challenges, huge setbacks, and heart breaking disappointments. Each of these circumstances will disguise themselves as failure. To be successful you must reject this lie and continue on towards your dream with even more determination.

Tough times require a strong WHY to prevail. The more difficult your obstacles are to overcome, the more you must keep your reasons for succeeding in front of you. Each time life knocks you down, you must bounce back with an even greater hunger to succeed.

Perseverance is the key to successful relationships, business endeavors, and your spiritual walk. Resilience and determination arise out of the depths of one's own heart. If your talent is just average or ordinary, your persistence and work ethic must become legendary. In order to bring your dreams alive you must carry a stubborn tenacity into the ring that will not concede to any other outcome than the one you set out for.

Endurance is faith being proven day in and day out. True believers are able to endure, because they believe in a God that won't let them down. Faith allows them to dig deeper and conquer their own doubts and fears. Step by step, they just keep pressing towards the prize.

There are no limits to what you can achieve except the ones you believe. Realism leads to a life of mediocrity and bondage while optimism leads to a life of greatness and freedom. To be a super achiever you must raise your standards, believe for more, and trust that God will bring it about.

On the way to success, there will be many times when you feel crushed, exhausted, and alone. You will be tempted to lay down, throw in the towel, and quit, but it's then mighty warrior that you must arise to the occasion. Your choices during these soul searching moments will ultimately define you. Refuse to be a victim and claim the crown of glory by way of persistence. Keep applying pressure until the universe folds to your demands. Have faith, stand strong, and press on…. for with God you are blessed and unstoppable!

Positive Affirmation:
I will never quit on myself or my dreams. I'm a champion, strategically designed to overcome adversity. I've been anointed by God to succeed therefore I am blessed and unstoppable!

Self-Assessment Questions:

What are some of the reasons behind my wanting to succeed in life?

What are my biggest challenges right now?

Is my WHY strong enough to overcome these obstacles?

When in the past did I face adversity, but refused to quit?

What helped me endure and keep pushing forward?

Who do I know that best exemplifies the heart and determination it takes to succeed?

If I quit every time things get rough will I ever be the person God made me to be?

What kind of music really inspires me to press on?

What are some of the movies that really motivate me to succeed?

How does my faith strengthen me during difficult times?

Who are some of the people who encourage me to persevere when I face trials in my life?

Who do I know that is really struggling right now that could use my help and encouragement?

Today's Prayer:

Thank you, Father, for giving me the strength to overcome and endure all the obstacles in my life. Help me to persevere even when things seem destined to fail. I know in my heart that nothing that I will ever face is greater than you. May the glory always be yours in Jesus' name. Amen.

Success Quotes:

It does not matter how slowly you go as long as you do not stop.
—Confucius

Let me not pray to be sheltered from dangers, but to be fearless in facing them. Let me not beg for the stilling of my pain, but for the heart to conquer it.
—Rabindranath Tagore

The difference between a successful person and others is not a lack of strength, not a lack of knowledge, but rather a lack in will.
—Vince Lombardi Jr.

Most of the important things in the world have been accomplished by people who have kept on trying when there seemed to be no hope at all.
—Dale Carnegie

I am not concerned that you have fallen -- I am concerned that you arise.
—Abraham Lincoln

One difference between those who make it and those who don't--regardless of their field of endeavor--is not the "talent" difference. Those who go over the top have a dream and the dream has them. They make the commitment and pursue that dream with dogged patience and persistence. Commitment produces consistent, enthusiastic effort that inevitably produces greater and greater rewards.
—Zig Ziglar

Nothing great is ever achieved without much enduring.
—Catherine of Siena

I am sore wounded but not slain, I will lay me down and bleed a while and then rise up to fight again.
—John Dryden

The difference between perseverance and obstinacy is that one comes from a strong will and the other from a strong won't.
—Henry Ward Beecher

Let me tell you something you already know. The world ain't all sunshine and rainbows. It's a very mean and nasty place and I don't care how tough you are it will beat you to your knees and keep you there permanently if you let it. You, me, or nobody is gonna hit as hard as life. But it ain't about how hard ya hit. It's about how hard you can get it and keep moving forward. How much you can take and keep moving forward. That's how winning is done!
—Rocky Balboa (Sylvester Stallone)

When you start living the life of your dreams, there will always be obstacles, doubters, mistakes and setbacks along the way. But with hard work, perseverance and self-belief there is no limit to what you can achieve.
—Roy T. Bennett

In the sympathy of Christ we find a sustaining power.
—Charles Haddon Spurgeon

It's not that I'm so smart, it's just that I stay with problems longer.
—Albert Einstein

Success seems to be largely a matter of hanging on after others have let go.
—William Feather

We will either find a way or make one.
—Hannibal

It always seems impossible until it's done.
—Nelson Mandela

A winner is just a loser who tried one more time.
—George M. Moore Jr.

Every strike brings me closer to the next home run.
—Babe Ruth

Let me tell you the secret that has led to my goal. My strength lies solely in my tenacity.
—Louis Pasteur

Perseverance is a great element of success. If you only knock long enough and loud enough at the gate, you are sure to wake up somebody.
—Henry Wadsworth Longfellow

The most essential factor is persistence – the determination never to allow your energy or enthusiasm to be dampened by the discouragement that must inevitably come.
—James Whitcomb Riley

Victory is always possible for the person who refuses to stop fighting.
—Napoleon Hill

Your Action Steps:
1. Pull out your WHY and remind yourself of all the reasons you must succeed.
2. Create an environment that breeds perseverance. (Listen to music that motivates you, watch videos that inspire you, and read books that encourage you to keep pushing on.)
3. Remove failure and all its synonyms from your vocabulary.
4. Stop focusing on how big your obstacles are and just zoom in on what needs to be done today.

Inspiration For Victory:
You are a survivor, God's most prized possession. Always remember He will never leave you nor forsake you!

— Day Twenty-Seven —
TAKE THE LIMITS OFF OF GOD

Bible Verse:
Now unto him that is able to do exceeding abundantly above all that we ask or think, according to the power that worketh in us.
Ephesians 3:20

You can tell the level of faith a person has by the size of their dreams. True believers dream bigger and aim higher for they know the size of the God they serve. If you want to accomplish amazing things and experience all that life has to offer, you must set enormous, almost to the edge of insanity, goals for yourself. The age of being practical is over. Dreaming with boldness takes the limits off of God and allows Him to work the miracles he is so willing to do.

Audacious ambitions create energy, stir up excitement, and build enthusiasm. Big dreams force you to explore the inner depths of your own creative power. When you reach for the impossible you have to amplify your thinking and aggressively expand your means. Those who scale down their goals become average achievers who choke on mediocrity. Your talents and gifts will not thrive in this kind of restricted environment. Passion was never designed to survive in an undersized cage. Your spirit craves expansion, longing to become all that Heaven made it to be.

The art of thinking big should make you feel very uncomfortable. If you're not uneasy about the size of your future, then you need to set the bar higher. Take all your goals and multiply them by ten (in this business world, we call this "10xing"). It's not your targets that are important here, it's what you're going to have to become in order to reach them. 10xing your objectives will stretch you to your limits and instigate growth.

Reach for the unreachable. Strive for the unattainable. When you are living in the center of your divine assignment all things are possible. The blessing and anointing on you makes all things obtainable. The God who gave you the dream is real, therefore whatever you imagine you can achieve inside your calling is realistic.

To manifest the incredible you must increase the level of your actions to that which is required to achieve greatness. 10xing demands that you raise your intensity to that of a champion. It will insist that you implement a strong discipline and strict regimen for success. Be hungry, dedicated, and fearless from the moment you open your eyes to the moment you close them.

Now's the time to step out in faith and believe! Refuse to let the masses keep you in the comfort zone. Use your gifts to chase what inspires you, with the full belief that you will attain it. Live the fantasy until it becomes your reality. The moment that you set your sights higher is the moment that you start really living. Whether your goal is to launch a business, play professional sports, or become a pop star, dreaming big is the only way to go.

Positive Affirmation:
I refuse to live a life of average. From this day forward, I will set massive 10x goals that excite and motivate me to push harder. Each day I will set out to do what the world says is impossible.

Self-Assessment Questions:

Have I set my goals massive enough?

Do these ambitions force me to stretch and grow?

What about my life do I have to change in order to reach them?

Do these goals really stir me up on the inside?

Am I in my calling doing what God has anointed me to do?

In what ways am I limiting God?

When I tell others about my dreams do they think I'm insane?

Did I raise my targets just a little higher or did I really 10x them?

What would my life be like if I achieve them?

Am I willing to commit to doing the action needed to bring them about?

Do I feel more excited about waking up in the morning now that I have these goals?

Do I believe in my heart that God will help me do this?

Have I placed God in a box that limits Him from moving the way he wants to in my life?

Are my goals set at worldly levels or at kingdom levels?

Today's Prayer:
Father, I pray today that you would show me how to take the limits off of you. Help me to dream bigger and believe in the wonderful things you have planned for my future. Give me the strength to aim higher and the faith needed to accomplish it in Jesus' name. Amen.

Success Quotes:

Have goals so big your problems pale in comparison.
—Grant Cardone

Every great dream begins with a dreamer. Always remember, you have within you the strength, the patience, and the passion to reach for the stars to change the world.
—Harriet Tubman

Deep into that darkness peering, long I stood there, wondering, fearing, doubting, dreaming dreams no mortal ever dared to dream before.
—Edgar Allan Poe

Dream no small dreams for they have no power to move the hearts of men.
—Johann Wolfgang von Goethe

If a little dreaming is dangerous, the cure for it is not to dream less but to dream more, to dream all the time.
—Marcel Proust

Winners, I am convinced, imagine their dreams first. They want it with all their heart and expect it to come true. There is, I believe, no other way to live.
—Joe Montana

It may be that those who do most, dream most.
—Stephen Butler Leacock

All successful people men and women are big dreamers. They imagine what their future could be, ideal in every respect, and then they work every day toward their distant vision, that goal or purpose.
—Brian Tracy

Don't live down to expectations. Go out there and do something remarkable.
—Wendy Wasserstein

Never give up on what you really want to do. The person with big dreams is more powerful than the one with all the facts.
—H. Jackson Brown, Jr.

Life is short, live bold! Be heard, be you, dream big, take risks, don't wait.
—Misty Gibbs

> **Your Action Steps:**
> Examine each area of your life to see if you have limited God from doing what He really wants to do for you? If you can accomplish your goals with your own talents and abilities it means you have forgotten to include God into the equation. Raise your targets drastically higher so that God has room to show up and show out in your life. Start asking big, dreaming big, and believing big and you will be amazed at how God starts to move in your life!

> **Inspiration For Victory:**
> **Don't settle for less than the incredible life God has planned for you!**

— Day Twenty-Eight —
LEARN THE ART OF COMMUNICATION

Bible Verse:
Let your speech always be gracious, seasoned with salt, so that you may know how you ought to answer each person.
Colossians 4:6

Communication is the art and exchange of one's thoughts, feelings, or ideas. The level of life that you experience will be determined by the quality and depth of the interactions you have. Learning to effectively communicate is crucial to building and maintaining strong relationships. Whether it's in business, love, or your personal life, being able to <u>connect</u> and clearly convey one's message is imperative to living a blessed life.

The most important key to communication is listening. Always seek first to discern the needs and concerns of others before interjecting your own. Being slow to speak and quick to listen allows you to accurately digest other people's viewpoints. This requires being focused and actively engaged, not just thinking of your next response. Don't just listen to the words they are saying, detect the emotions behind them. Pay close attention to their tone, body language, and nonverbal expressions. Your goal is to gain a deep understanding of their world and how they see things.

All too often, messages get lost in the translation. Successful dialogue hinges on precise and accurate interpretation. Make sure that you fully comprehend what the other person is trying to express and that you are receiving it as intended. This will help prevent any conflicts, arguments, or misunderstandings from arising.

To become a powerful communicator one must develop a personal connection with the listener. Doing this requires acknowledging them, validating their opinions, and searching for some type of common ground between you. Finding out what's important to them builds rapport and makes them a lot more receptive to what you have to say. The more trust you establish with the person, the better the relationship is going to be.

As Christians, we are to guard our mouths from all forms of corrupt communication. When we converse with others, we should always speak with grace, love, and respect. Every word should be crafted with the kindness, meekness, and gentleness Christ best exemplified.

We all come from different places, cultures, and backgrounds, which makes us all wired differently. What we say to one person could have a totally different meaning to someone else. It's essential not just to speak in ways that we are comfortable with, but take those that we are speaking to into consideration. Effective communication is a learned skill that anyone can master. The more you practice and interact with others the better you will become at it.

> **Positive Affirmation:**
> I am a master communicator who listens and acknowledges all those that I interact with. I seek first to fully understand the views and concerns of others before I express mine. Each word I carefully craft so that no corrupt communication proceeds out of my mouth.

Self-Assessment Questions:

When interacting with others do I tend to engage more in talking or listening?

Do I acknowledge those that I talk to making them feel heard and understood?

When people are talking to me, am I really listening or just thinking of my next response?

Do I have a habit of interrupting people before they finish what they are trying to say?

How often do I find myself saying things that I later regret?

How often do I find myself regretting something I didn't say?

Do I find it easy or challenging to articulate my ideas to others?

How important is communication in my profession?

How important is communication in my personal relationships?

Do I respect the views of other people or is mine the only one that matters?

In what ways can I improve my communication skills?

Do I speak in a language or communication style that my listener can understand?

How does it feel when someone really listens to understand me?

Todays' Prayer:

Father, I pray today that you would make me a more effective listener. Help me to become a powerful communicator so that I can articulate in the perfect language style of my listener. Grant me the wisdom and discernment to know when to speak and when to just listen in Jesus name. Amen.

Success Quotes:

Let no corrupting talk come out of your mouths, but only such as is good for building up, as fits the occasion, that it may give grace to those who hear.
—Ephesians 4:29

The way we communicate with others and with ourselves ultimately determines the quality of our lives.
—Tony Robbins

Speak clearly, if you speak at all; carve every word before you let it fall.
—Oliver Wendell Holmes, Sr.

Take advantage of every opportunity to practice your communication skills so that when important occasions arise, you will have the gift, the style, the sharpness, the clarity, and the emotions to affect other people.
—Jim Rohn

Genius is the ability to put into effect what is on your mind.
—F. Scott Fitzgerald

Developing excellent communication skills is absolutely essential to effective leadership. The leader must be able to share knowledge and ideas to transmit a sense of urgency and enthusiasm to others. If a leader can't get a message across clearly and motivate others to act on it, then having a message doesn't even matter.
—Gilbert Amelio

You can have brilliant ideas, but if you can't get them across, your ideas won't get you anywhere.
—Lee Iacocca

The art of communication is the language of leadership.
—James Humes

The most important thing in communication is hearing what isn't said.
—Peter Drucker

Think like a wise man but communicate in the language of the people.
—William Butler Yeats

Wise men talk because they have something to say; fools, because they have to say something.
—Plato

Give me the gift of a listening heart.
—King Solomon

I won a nickname, "The Great Communicator." But I never thought it was my style or the words I used that made a difference: It was the content. I wasn't a great communicator, but I communicated great things, and they didn't spring full bloom from my brow, they came from the heart of a great nation from our experience, our wisdom, and our belief in principles that have guided us for two centuries.
—President Ronald Reagan

You can make more friends in two months by becoming interested in other people than you can in two years by trying to get other people interested in you.
—Dale Carnegie

Courage is what it takes to stand up and speak; courage is also what it takes to sit down and listen.
—Winston Churchill

Trust is the glue of life. It's the most essential ingredient in effective communication. It's the foundational principle that holds all relationships.
—Stephen Covey

Assumptions are barriers to effective communication both at home and in the work place.
—Annie Armen

Communication – the human connection – is the key to personal and career success.
—Paul J. Meyer

Most of the successful people I've known are the ones who do more listening than talking.
—Bernard Baruch

Communication is the solvent of all problems, therefore communication skills are the foundation for personal development.
—Peter Shepherd

As a company grows, communication becomes its biggest challenge.
—Ben Horowitz

Language creates reality. Words have power. Speak always to create joy.
—Deepak Chopra

It's not what you tell them…it's what they hear.
—Red Auerbach

Talk to people about themselves and they will listen for hours.
—Benjamin Disraeli

It is better to keep one's mouth shut and be thought a fool than to open it and resolve all doubt.
—Abraham Lincoln

Open communication is the lifeblood that keeps a marriage in the spring and summer seasons- times of optimism and enjoyment.
—Gary Chapman

To be a successful communicator, you need to focus on fundamental principles rather than small superficial things.
—Bill Calhoun

You never know when a moment and a few sincere words can have an impact on a life.
—Zig Ziglar

> **Your Action Steps:**
> In order to establish a strong connection with someone, you must first display that you are truly interested in them as a person. Today, when engaging in conversations, make it your focus to really <u>listen</u> to the person you are speaking with. Ask open ended questions that will stimulate the dialogue back and forth between the two of you. Using reflective listening will ensure the other person that he or she is in an environment where they can be fully heard, supported, and understood. Give them your complete attention and make them feel as though they are the most important person in the world to you at that moment. This will allow you to bond quicker and connect on a much deeper level.

> **Inspiration For Victory:**
> # God will go above and beyond to rain down his incredible blessings on you!

— Day Twenty-Nine —
ALIGN WITH GRATITUDE

Bible Verse:
In everything give thanks; for this is God's will for you in Christ Jesus.
1 Thessalonians 5:18

Start today off with aligning yourself with the power of gratitude. The first thing you should do every morning and the last thing you should do every evening is to cultivate a spirit of thankfulness. Express your appreciation to your Father in heaven and praise him for the mighty things he has done in your life. Praise him for the future blessings he is about to bestow on you.

No matter what challenging circumstances you might be facing, there are many things that you should be grateful for. Aligning with thankfulness will guide your mental state back to the Now. This will immediately bring both your mind and emotions back into order.

Thankfulness generates a magnetic vibration that cancels out the destructive forces of negativity. When you release it into an environment, it immediately begins to raise and uplift the level of consciousness. People can sense this energy and are attracted to its underlying current. The more you hold that positive state, the more powerful it becomes.

Gratitude is an invisible factory that manufactures and multiplies more situations and outcomes that regenerate its own existence. When you truly appreciate the things you currently have in your life, you send out an invitation for more of these miracles and blessings to manifest into physical reality. Some doors of opportunity can only be accessed with gratitude and without the key of thankfulness they will stay shut forever.

Sincere gratitude will positively impact every aspect of your being. Let everyone around you know just how grateful you are to have them in your life, it will be a huge difference maker. Stir up sincere appreciation, until you can feel it flowing through every cell in your body. Radiate with thanksgiving and maintain this mindset consistently throughout your day. Commit right now to a life of genuine gratitude and you will be amazed at the astonishing results!

> **Positive Affirmation:**
> I am so grateful for the wonderful people and blessings radiating in my life. I am so thankful for the everyday miracles that I get to be a part of. I am so blessed!

Self-Assessment Questions:

Who in my life am I most grateful for right now?

How can I maintain a consistent state of gratitude in all circumstances?

How can I openly express my thankfulness for the people I have in my life today?

What kind of feelings do I feel inside when I am grateful?

What is the body language of a person who is truly appreciative and thankful to be alive?

Who do I need to call right now and share my gratitude with?

What is the greatest experience I have ever had in my life?

What talents do I have that I am most grateful for?

What about my health am I most thankful for?

What past experiences am I most grateful to have been a part of?

Who in my life most symbolizes the spirit of gratitude?

Do I feel better when I am in a state of complaining or when I am in a state of thankfulness?

In which of these two above states do I have more energy?

> **Today's Prayer:**
> I pray today, Father, for you to help me maintain a sense of thankfulness in all situations. Make me a shining light of gratitude and praise. Help me show all those around me just how thankful I am to have them in my life in Jesus' name. Amen.

Success Quotes:

Feeling gratitude and not expressing it is like wrapping a present & not giving it.
—William Arthur Ward

Gratitude is heaven itself.
—William Blake

Gratitude unlocks the fullness of life. It turns what we have into enough, & more. It turns denial into acceptance, chaos to order, confusion to clarity. It can turn a meal into a feast, a house into a home, a stranger into a friend. Gratitude makes sense of our past, brings peace for today, & creates a vision for tomorrow.
—Melody Beattie

Enjoy the little things, for one day you may look back & realize they were the big things.
—Robert Brault

Cultivate the habit of being grateful for every good thing that comes to you, and to give thanks continuously. And because all things have contributed to your advancement, you should include all things in your gratitude.
—Ralph Waldo Emerson

Let gratitude be the pillow upon which you kneel to say your nightly prayer. And let faith be the bridge you build to overcome evil and welcome good.
—Maya Angelou

Gratitude is not only the greatest of virtues, but the parent of all others.
—Cicero

When you are grateful, fear disappears and abundance appears.
—Anthony Robbins

The unthankful heart discovers no mercies; but the thankful heart will find, in every hour, some heavenly blessings.
—Henry Ward Beecher

Your Actions Steps:
Today focus on all the wonderful things in your life. Give God sincere praise for the awesome things he has done for you in the past, the miracles he's doing in your present, and the unbelievable plans he has for your future. Think about all the amazing people he brought across your path and the precious moments you experienced together. Let them all know just how special they are to you and how much better your life is because of them.

Inspiration For Victory:
Your best days are not over, God is just getting started with you!

— Day Thirty —
BECOME A PRAYER WARRIOR

Bible Verse:
And the Lord restored the fortunes of Job, when he had prayed for his friends. And the Lord gave Job twice as much as he had before.
Job 42:10

The greatest gift you can give to the world is prayer. Interceding for others releases Heaven's blessings on both you and the person you are praying for. The more you pray, the more you allow the Holy Spirit to intervene in your life and in the lives of those around you.

Prayer is not the same thing as wishing or hoping for something to happen, it's knowing fully in your heart that it will. The power of intercession is only equivalent to the belief behind it. Prayer is not a stand-alone principle, it must be applied in tandem with the principle of faith in order to be truly effective.

If there's an area in your own life where you are struggling, praying for someone facing the same challenges as you will initiate your own healing process. When you intercede for others, your spirit and emotional state will begin to shift back into a state of balance. It redirects your focus off yourself and onto your spiritual calling of loving others.

Each day your heavenly Father will place people in your path that need you to pray for them. These individuals have been specifically assigned to you and it's your job to petition for them. Praying for others allows God the opportunity to make himself known to unbelievers and it also strengthens his relationship with those who have already accepted him.

Whenever you feel moved to petition for someone, do it immediately without hesitation. Communicate with your Father like you would an intimate friend or family member. If you are unsure as to what the particular need is, just ask for God's perfect will to be manifested in their life. Requests offered up this way will fall on open ears. You don't have to pray some long drawn out prayer for God to hear you, just speak from the heart and believe.

Prayer can shift the dynamics of any situation you direct it to. The physical distance between you and the one you are praying for doesn't matter. This means you have the ability to impact the world from right where you are at. No matter what the situation or how sever the circumstance your prayer will make a difference!

> **Positive Affirmation:**
> I am a prayer warrior in the army of Almighty God. I'm constantly interceding on the behalf of those around me. I pray boldly for the needs of others and unbelievable miracles happen!

Self-Assessment Questions:

What are the type of prayers God always answers?

Do I pray for myself more than I pray for others?

How can I be more aware of the needs of those around me?

Who do I know that needs intercession right now?

Do I trust and believe that God will answer my petitions for them?

How would Jesus want me to pray for them?

How do I feel inside when I am interceding on the behalf of others?

Who are some people with strong faith that I could assemble a prayer team with?

What are some instances in the past where God has answered my prayers?

Where is my focus when I am making requests for those in need? What's the differences between wishing, hoping, and praying? When my prayers are answered, am I making sure that God gets all the glory?

> **Today's Prayer:**
> Father, I pray today that you would send people into my life that need prayer. Heighten my sense of awareness so that I know exactly what I should be petitioning for. Help me to make these requests known to you with the highest level of faith. May your will be done always in Jesus' name. Amen.

Success Quotes:

God is looking for people to use, and if you can get usable, he will wear you out. The most dangerous prayer you can pray is this: Use me.
—Rick Warren

The function of prayer is not to influence God, but rather to change the nature of the one who prays.
—Soren Kierkegaard

Prayer becomes more meaningful as we counsel with the Lord in all of our doings, as we express heartfelt gratitude, and as we pray for others.
—David A. Bednar

Pray for someone else's child, your pastor, the military, the police officers, the firemen, the teachers, the government. There's no end to the ways that you can intervene on behalf of others through prayer.
—Monica Johnson

In doing God's work, there is no substitute for praying. The men of prayer cannot be displaced with other kinds of men.
—Edward McKendree Bounds

I have been benefited by praying for others; for by making an errand to God for them I have gotten something for myself.
—Samuel Rutherford

The man who mobilizes the Christian church to pray will make the greatest contribution to world evangelization in history.
—Andrew Murray

Prayer does not fit us for the greater work; prayer is the greater work.
—Oswald Chambers.

To be a Christian without prayer is no more possible than to be alive without breathing.
—Martin Luther

Prayer is man's greatest power!
—W. Clement Stone

> **Your Action Steps:**
> Interceding for others is a powerful weapon that ushers in change. In whatever area of your life you are struggling with most, find someone with similar challenges and pray for God to help them overcome it. Every time you feel angry, frustrated, or discouraged by what you are going through, search for someone in need that you can intercede for.

> **Inspiration For Victory:**
> **Bold prayers activate the power of God. Trust him to intervene on your behalf!**

— Day Thirty-One —
IMPACT LIVES DAILY

Bible Verse:
And Jesus called them to him and said to them, "You know that those who are considered rulers of the Gentiles lord it over them, and their great ones exercise authority over them. But it shall not be so among you. But whoever would be great among you must be your servant, and whoever would be first among you must be slave of all. For even the Son of Man came not to be served but to serve, and to give his life as a ransom for many."
Mark 10: 42-45

Authentic success is not about accumulation, it's about positively impacting lives. The level at which you do this will ultimately become your own legacy. God has planted gifts and talents in you that you are to share with the world. People who need exactly what you have been given to give will be sent to you by the divine. Each opportunity will be a chance for you to make a difference, just be aware when the situation arises and do your part.

The real purpose behind becoming successful is having the means and resources to help more and more people. The more you give the more that will be entrusted to you. Jesus gave the world the perfect example of a life based solely around servanthood. He laid his own life down for us. The greatest leaders know that leadership is only born through sacrifice. They lay down their own needs in exchange for their team and comrades.

Self-centeredness is in our nature, but to live and experience a life of complete fulfillment we must overcome that nature. You will never feel more alive than when you freely give. By pouring out yourself through acts of kindness, love, and compassion you will tap into the states of nirvana. Find ways to connect your passions, to making people's lives better. Every day, filter all your actions through the question: *Am I making a difference in people's lives?* This will change the whole dynamic of your life. When you shift from a selfish state of consciousness to that of servanthood, your reach and circle of influence will begin to expand way beyond measure.

God has empowered you to change the world. Feed the hungry, clothe the poor, and comfort the broken. Inspire those who are empty. Encourage those who are on the verge of giving up. Stand up against injustice. Shake the world by doing good deeds daily. Sometimes just a smile or a random act of kindness can make all the difference in the world to someone who is on the verge of collapse.

The quickest way to receive a miracle is become one for someone else. True freedom arises when life is detached from acquiring and consumerism to one of true usefulness to others. Give just to give, love just to love, serve just to serve. Your treasure map lies in the struggling people around you. When you assist people in their time of need, a part of you lives on in them forever. Love is not meant to be hoarded, but to be constantly displayed in action through the act of service to others. If you're not really giving, you're not really living. The seats at the top are reserved for individuals who impact lives. Through service you will add genuine value to the world, conquer success, and add real meaning to your own life.

Positive Affirmation:
I vow to make my life one of servanthood. I give just to give, love just to love, and serve just to serve. The purpose of my life is to positively impact the lives of others.

Self-Assessment Questions:

What does servanthood mean to me?

How can I serve more people?

How would helping and giving to others improve my life?

What times can I recall in the past that I truly gave to others expecting and wanting nothing in return?

How does helping others feel inside?

Who do I know that is truly living a life of servanthood?

What talents did God plant inside me that I am to freely share with others?

Who is the one person I have helped the most in my life?

What kind of legacy do I want to leave here on earth?

What positive effects have I witnessed from someone giving?

When in the past could I have helped more?

In what ways can I use my current influence to positively make a difference?

Who around me really needs my help right now?

How can I place myself in an environment that gives me more opportunities to impact people's lives?

Today's Prayer:

Lord, I pray that you will pour out a true spirit of servanthood over my life. Help me to give in unselfish ways so that I can make the biggest impact possible. Thank you for giving me daily opportunities to make a difference in Jesus' name. Amen.

Success Quotes:

No one has ever become poor by giving.
—Anne Frank

The purpose of life is not to be happy. It is to be useful, to be honorable, to be compassionate to have it make some difference that you have lived and lived well.
—Ralph Waldo Emerson

There is no exercise better for the heart than reaching down and lifting people up.
—John Holmes

You have not lived today until you have done something for someone who can never repay you.
—John Bunyan

Those who are happiest are those who do the most for others.
—Booker T. Washington

Even the smallest act of caring for another person is like a drop of water –it will make ripples throughout the entire pond.
—Jessy and Bryan Matteo

Self-improvement comes mainly from trying to help others.
—Sir John Templeton

We can have anything we want on life, if we just help others to find what they need.
—Ebelsain Villegas

If you're not making someone else's life better, then you're wasting your time. Your life will become better by making other lives better.
—Will Smith

We are healed to help others. We are blessed to be a blessing. We are saved to serve, not to sit around and wait for heaven.
—Rick Warren

The purpose of life is to contribute in some way to making things better.
—Robert F. Kennedy

I am only one, but I am one. I cannot do everything, but I can do something. And I will not let what I cannot do interfere with what I can do.
—Edward Everett Hale

> **Your Action Steps:**
> Every day make it a priority to sow positive seeds of hope and encouragement into the lives of those around you. It doesn't require much to show love and kindness to people going through difficulties, but the impact can be huge. Your support could mean everything to someone who is hurting, in distress, or feeling alone. Yield to God's guidance and He will show you exactly what to say or do in each situation.

> **Inspiration For Victory:**
> **God has empowered you to become someone's miracle!**

BLESSED AND UNSTOPPABLE

THE SELF-AWARENESS WORKBOOK

SELF-AWARENESS

Self-Awareness is having the ability to see yourself as you really are. It's being able to honestly assess your natural strengths, weaknesses, passions, talents, and abilities without personal bias. Self-Awareness helps you better understand who your are, what your calling is, when to pursue it, why you are doing it, and where to do it so that you can effectively position yourself for success.

DETOX EMOTIONALLY

Write down the names of the people who have hurt you in the past. Pray over this list of names and ask God to bless them tremendously in every aspect of their lives.

_____
_____
_____
_____
_____
_____
_____
_____
_____
_____
_____

Do this every day until you flush all the negative energy and ill will towards these people out of your system.

GRATITUDE

Who in my life am I most grateful for?

_____
_____
_____
_____

What are some of the things in my life that I am most thankful for?

_____
_____
_____
_____
_____

What are some of the experiences that I have had in the past that I am most appreciative of?

_____
_____
_____
_____

SELF-AWARENESS

What are my passions, interests, and hobbies etc.?

_____
_____
_____

What are my talents, gifts, and natural abilities?

_____
_____
_____
_____
_____

PASSION
INTERESTS
HOBBIES
TALENTS GIFTS
ABILITIES

What do other people tell me I'm good at?

_____
_____
_____
_____

MY CORE VALUES

What are my top 7 personal core values?
(For Example: wisdom, truth, faith, love, peace, kindness, excellence, etc.)

1._____
2._____
3._____
4._____
5._____
6._____
7._____

The things on this list should be what you want your life to stand for and what you most want your life to represent. Once you have your core values written out, examine each area of your life to make sure you are in alignment with them. From this point forward, filter all your life decisions through this list.

SELF-AWARENESS

What are my biggest strengths?
1._____
2._____
3._____
4._____
5._____

What are my weaknesses?
1._____
2._____
3._____
4._____
5._____

How can I make my strengths even stronger?
_____
_____

How can I transform my weaknesses into strengths?
_____
_____
_____

LEGACY

What do I want my legacy to be?
_____
_____
_____
_____

What do I want them to write about me in my obituary?
_____
_____
_____
_____

How do I want my headstone/grave marker to read?
_____
_____
_____

DEFINE SUCCESS

How do I define success?

_____
_____

What do I have to accomplish in my own life in order to feel successful?

WHAT DOES SUCCESS MEAN TO ME?

_____
_____
_____

In what ways can I bless others when I become successful?

_____
_____
_____

SELF-AWARENESS

What five words best describe who I am right now?
1._____
2._____
3._____
4._____
5._____

What five words best describe who I want to be?
1._____
2._____
3._____
4._____
5._____

What words do I want people to use when describing me?
1._____
2._____
3._____

WHAT'S MY WHY?

What are the top 10 reasons I want to be successful?

1. _____
2. _____
3. _____
4. _____
5. _____
6. _____
7. _____
8. _____
9. _____
10. _____

Out of this list of ten, which three inspire and motivate me the most? (Together, these three are your *why*.)

1. _____
2. _____
3. _____

(Is my why strong enough to carry me through the tough times?)

MY INNER CIRCLE

Who are the five people I associate with the most?
1._____
2._____
3._____
4._____
5._____

Grade their impact on your life from one to five, with one being the most negative and five representing the most positive?
1._____
2._____
3._____
4_____
5._____

What's the sum total grade for my inner circle?_____

Begin immediately to distance yourself from anyone who grades out at one or two. If they grade as a three, which is neutral, find a way to improve the dynamic of the relationship. When the sum total of your team of five finally grades out at twenty or better, you've built a strong inner circle of positive and trust worthy people you can achieve success with.

MY INNER CIRCLE

Understanding The Inner Circle Grading System:

Inner Circle Grade of 5-14: Any total sum score grading under 15 is a serious issue and must be addressed immediately. Your inner circle at this state is a major liability. These type of associations **will not** produce an environment conducive for success.

Inner Circle Grade of 15-19: Any total sum score grading out at 15-19 is a sign that your inner circle is not hindering your success, but at the same time is not necessarily helping you either. These type of associations produce mediocre results and give way to an average everyday existence. The majority of the world have inner circles that grade out at this level.

Inner Circle Grade of 20-25: Any total sum score grading out at 20-25 means that you have a strong supporting cast around you. People who have these types of inner circles have a much greater chance at reaching their full potential and achieving higher levels of success. This is the inner circle of great leaders, champions, and innovators who end up making a real difference in the world.

Important note: Success is a TEAM sport. If you do not have at least five people in your inner circle, it's a sign that you are isolated and closed off from the world. This will limit your success just as much as associating with the wrong people. Start looking for strong and positive influences to surround yourself with who will fully support you and your dreams.

MY WISE COUNSEL

Who are my mentors?
1._____
2._____
3._____
4._____
5._____

Who do I go to for advice and wise counsel?
1._____
2._____
3._____
4._____
5._____

Who would be a great addition to my team of advisors?
1._____
2._____
3._____

MY BUCKET LIST

What are the top 20 things I want to do or experience in my lifetime?

1. _____
2. _____
3. _____
4. _____
5. _____
6. _____
7. _____
8. _____
9. _____
10. _____
11. _____
12. _____
13. _____ 17. _____
14. _____ 18. _____
15. _____ 19. _____
16. _____ 20. _____

BLESSED AND UNSTOPPABLE

BRINGING YOUR LIFE INTO FOCUS

YOUR NORTH STAR

Write the vision, and make it plain upon tables, that he may run that readeth it.
Habakkuk 2:2

Vision: What a person/company/organization wants to be. It paints a powerful and inspiring picture of what the future will look like.

Mission: Why a person/company/organization exists in the first place. It should be a clear and concise statement short enough to fit on a T-shirt.

Core Values: What a person/company/organization stands for.

Slogan: A catchy phrase that effectively describes a person/company/organization. It's a strong tag line that articulates a brief representation of the entity and makes it more memorable.

Long Term Aspirations: A person/company/organization's top outcomes desired for years to come. It's more than just goals it's the consequences, results, and after effects of actually achieving them.

YOUR NORTH STAR

What's your Vision?

What's your Mission?

What are your 7 Core Values?

What's your Slogan?

What are your Long Term Aspirations?

SHORT TERM GOALS

AREA OF MY LIFE	THIS WEEK (My Top 3)	NEXT WEEK (My Top 3)	THIS MONTH (My Top 3)
HEALTH			
FAMILY			
MARRIAGE			
SPIRITUAL			
FINANCES			
FRIENDS			
BUSINESS			
IMPACT			

MID-TERM GOALS

AREA OF MY LIFE	3 MONTHS (My Top 3)	6 MONTHS (My Top 3)	12 WEEKS (My Top 3)
HEALTH			
FAMILY			
MARRIAGE			
SPIRITUAL			
FINANCES			
FRIENDS			
BUSINESS			
IMPACT			

LONG TERM GOALS

AREA OF MY LIFE	1 YEAR (My Top 3)	2-3 YEAR (My Top 3)	5 YEAR (My Top 3)
HEALTH			
FAMILY			
MARRIAGE			
SPIRITUAL			
FINANCES			
FRIENDS			
BUSINESS			
IMPACT			

MY TOP GOALS

	GOAL 1 (0:00-0:15)	GOAL 2 (0:15-0:30)	GOAL 3 (0:30-0:45)	GOAL 4 (0:45-1:00)
5 A.M.				
6 A.M.				
7 A.M.				
8 A.M.				
9 A.M.				
10 A.M.				
11 A.M.				
12 P.M.				
1 P.M.				
2 P.M.				
3 P.M.				
4 P.M.				
5 P.M.				

THIS WEEK'S GOALS

What are the most important tasks to accomplish this week that will actually bring me closer to my goals?

_____
_____

In what ways can I improve myself?

_____
_____

Who are the people I need to reach out to or connect with?

_____
_____

How can I strengthen my health this week?

_____
_____

Where do I need to place my focus, time, and energy?

_____
_____

BLESSED AND UNSTOPPABLE

WISDOM FOR ACHIEVING GREATNESS

POWERFUL WISDOM

1. To go to the next level, you must boldly attack the things that scare you.
#BillyAlsbrooks

2. Never look at defeat as permanent, but rather see it as temporary gestation period from which a greater victory will be born.
#BillyAlsbrooks

3. Love changes everything it touches.
#BillyAlsbrooks

4. Happiness chases those who master The Art of Forgiveness.
#BillyAlsbrooks

POWERFUL WISDOM

5. Truth doesn't discriminate, she blesses all who embrace her.
#BillyAlsbrooks

6. The first step to becoming a game changer is to be a peace with who you really are.
#BillyAlsbrooks

7. Doubt is the plague. Those around you infected with it must be quarantined!
#BillyAlsbrooks

8. Thoughts and behaviors consistently aligned with success will eventually translate into the outcomes that create it.
#BillyAlsbrooks

POWERFUL WISDOM

9. Make sure your business is rooted in truth, for truth expands naturally needing no trickery or manipulation to fulfill its purposes.
#BillyAlsbrooks

10. Wisdom has not been fully accepted until it is consistently applied.
#BillyAlsbrooks

11. Success is the offspring of previous thought that transpired into effective action.
#BillyAlsbrooks

12. Your life comes directly off the assembly line of your imagination.
#BillyAlsbrooks

POWERFUL WISDOM

13. Success derives out of self-awareness.
#BillyAlsbrooks

14. Once you awaken to the resources inside you, lack and scarcity will not be able to exist.
#BillyAlsbrooks

15. The quickest way to overcome failure is to starve yourself of the thoughts and actions that allow it to sustain itself.
#BillyAlsbrooks

16. Questions are your transportation. Certain questions you have asked yourself or didn't ask yourself led you to your current reality.
#BillyAlsbrooks

POWERFUL WISDOM

17. Truth is the best marketing strategy ever invented.
#BillyAlsbrooks

18. When you master the things under your control, the uncontrollable eventually becomes irrelevant.
#BillyAlsbrooks

19. Those who have gained revelation of the power within are not subject to life, life is subject to them.
#BillyAlsbrooks

20. Truth doesn't force itself on anyone it just sits there and waves.
#BillyAlsbrooks

POWERFUL WISDOM

21. Your thoughts are matches. You're only one thought away from setting the whole world on fire. One great idea can change your life forever.
#BillyAlsbrooks

22. Money should be seen as tool just like a carpenter's hammer. Use it to build and construct things that make a difference.
#BillyAlsbrooks

23. The level of success you experience will all hinge on your ability to stay focused.
#BillyAlsbrooks

24. The key to accomplishing the impossible is breaking it down into small daily steps that are possible.
#BillyAlsbrooks

POWERFUL WISDOM

25. There's nothing more attractive than a person comfortable in their own skin.
#BillyAlsbrooks

26. Some people were only meant to be in your life for a season. Conflict arises when you attempt to keep them around longer than destiny intended.
#BillyAlsbrooks

27. In the imagination lies an infinite world of possibilities. Those who live in her realm become the innovators that change the world.
#BillyAlsbrooks

28. Actions are the indisputable evidence of a corresponding mindset.
#BillyAlsbrooks

POWERFUL WISDOM

29. Schedule your day around the tasks that move you towards your goals. Hold every second of your life accountable to your success.
#BillyAlsbrooks

30. You are getting 80% of your results from 20% of your thinking. This means a small change in your thinking can translate into huge results.
#BillyAlsbrooks

31. You can only attract outcomes that are equivalent to the level of your consciousness.
#BillyAlsbrooks

32. Champions make adjustments not excuses.
#BillyAlsbrooks

POWERFUL WISDOM

33. Each level of success requires a different measure of consciousness, discipline, preparation, execution, and consistency.
#BillyAlsbrooks

34. Successful people are married to consistent execution. They don't practice until they get it right, they practice until they can't do it wrong.
#BillyAlsbrooks

35. To sustain success one must learn to evolve.
#BillyAlsbrooks

36. You cannot achieve massive success with mediocre habits.
#BillyAlsbrooks

POWERFUL WISDOM

37. Find out the most important things that determine success in your field and then devote all your time and energy to doing them.
#BillyAlsbrooks

38. The beginning of change starts with a shift in focus.
#BillyAlsbrooks

39. Prosperity comes to those who add value to people's lives.
#BillyAlsbrooks

40. Let your actions proclaim your allegiance to success.
#BillyAlsbrooks

POWERFUL WISDOM

41. Denial will continue to hold you hostage until you take responsibility for your actions. Ignoring the facts will not improve your circumstances.
#BillyAlsbrooks

42. We are in all in a state of evolution. Our consciousness is evolving towards full revelation of the one God who created us.
#BillyAlsbrooks

43. Faith, mind, and the spoken word are the three most powerful weapons in existence. When united in truth, NOTHING can prevail against them.
#BillyAlsbrooks

44. Each receives according to their awareness. All states of consciousness connect to the same power source, but with different levels of understanding.
#BillyAlsbrooks

POWERFUL WISDOM

45. Begging doesn't move God, faith does!
#BillyAlsbrooks

46. Right thinking sustained long enough will turn chaos into order.
#BillyAlsbrooks

47. Truth is the chiropractor of the mind.
#BillyAlsbrooks

48. The Law of Attraction is not about thinking positive thoughts, it's about projecting them.
#BillyAlsbrooks

POWERFUL WISDOM

49. Forgiveness is dialysis for the soul.
#BillyAlsbrooks

50. The masses earn money, the rich and wealthy create it.
#BillyAlsbrooks

51. Abraham Lincoln cannot emancipate you from your thinking, you must liberate yourself.
#BillyAlsbrooks

52. A disciplined mind, rooted in truth, can do the impossible.
#BillyAlsbrooks

POWERFUL WISDOM

53. When we walk in love, we align and unify with God.
#BillyAlsbrooks

54. Unforgiveness is volunteered emotional incarceration.
#BillyAlsbrooks

55. God's love is the science behind all creation.
#BillyAlsbrooks

56. Successful people master the basics. They become phenomenal by consistently doing the little things well.
#BillyAlsbrooks

POWERFUL WISDOM

57. Your faith activates the power within you, the spoken word releases it.
#BillyAlsbrooks

58. You cannot walk through the door to God's blessing still carrying every wrong done to you in the past.
#BillyAlsbrooks

59. Change will only happen when you initiate it.
#BillyAlsbrooks

60. Your mindset is the thermostat that sets the tone for every environment you enter.
#BillyAlsbrooks

POWERFUL WISDOM

61. To become successful you must seize and conquer every opportunity that presents itself.
#BillyAlsbrooks

62. Faith is the only language that the universe responds to.
#BillyAlsbrooks

63. What doubt murdered, faith can resurrect.
#BillyAlsbrooks

64. Champions discipline and condition their mind in such a way that it allows them to do the impossible.
#BillyAlsbrooks

POWERFUL WISDOM

65. Success is birthed out of submission. When we surrender to God's will, blessings begin to chase us down.
#BillyAlsbrooks

66. The way you think today will manufacture what you experience tomorrow.
#BillyAlsbrooks

67. Your destiny will be determined by the quality of questions you ask yourself.
#BillyAlsbrooks

68. Success requires boldness. You've got to be hungry, dedicated, and fearless from the moment you open your eyes to the moment you close them.
#BillyAlsbrooks

POWERFUL WISDOM

69. When you mix your passion with an insane work ethic, what other people say or think about you becomes irrelevant.
#BillyAlsbrooks

70. The moment that you start praying for others to be healed is the moment your own healing process begins.
#BillyAlsbrooks

71. Your life should be one great exhibition of doing the impossible.
#BillyAlsbrooks

72. Success can only be accessed through the gate of discipline.
#BillyAlsbrooks

POWERFUL WISDOM

73. Success must be first engineered in the mind.
#BillyAlsbrooks

74. Self-discipline is the bridge that connects dreams to reality.
#BillyAlsbrooks

75. When passion is married to singleness of purpose it produces the environment needed for greatness.
#BillyAlsbrooks

76. One by one you must overcome the daily temptations that stand against your dreams.
#BillyAlsbrooks

POWERFUL WISDOM

77. Success is a marathon of consistency.
#BillyAlsbrooks

78. Passion is the energy created when one is doing what God designed them to do.
#BillyAlsbrooks

79. The great salesmen don't get intimidated by the word no, they get motivated by it.
#BillyAlsbrooks

80. Perseverance transforms average everyday people into champions.
#BillyAlsbrooks

BLESSED AND UNSTOPPABLE

THE POWER TO OVERCOME

GOD HAS AN AMAZING PLAN FOR YOU

Many are the plans in the mind of a man, but it is the purpose of the Lord that will stand.
Proverbs 19:21

1. THE SEVEN ELEMENTS OF GOD'S PLAN

- Eternal Salvation **(John 10:27-29, 1 John 5:13)**
- Prosperity and Abundance **(Jeremiah 29:11, Psalms 112:1-3)**
- Complete Healing **(Matthew 4:23, Psalms 107:20, Isaiah 53:5)**
- Complete Restoration **(Joel 2:25-26, Zechariah 9:12)**
- Refinement **(Jeremiah 9:7, Psalms 66:10-12)**
- Peace That Passes All Understanding **(John 14:27, Romans 8:6)**
- A Kingdom Purpose with an Earthly Assignment **(Ephesians 4:11-12, Romans 8:28)**

2. GOD WILL PLANT A POWERFUL DREAM INSIDE YOU
(GENESIS 37:9, ACTS 2:17)

- There are many examples in the Bible of this: God gave Noah the dream of building an ark, Abraham the dream of being a father to a great nation, and Joseph the dream that he was going to be a ruler of a great nation.
- Your dream will have to go through God's Word in order to be achieved.
- Let there be no confusion about this, God will never plant a dream in you that contradicts his Word.

3. THE DREAM WILL GO WAY BEYOND YOUR OWN PERSONAL LIMITATIONS
(EPHESIANS 3:20, PHILIPPIANS 4:13)

- God doesn't call the equipped, He equips the ones that He calls.
- God's assignment will require your <u>absolute</u> faith in him.
- You are to draw from His power and His strength rather than your own.

4. GOD WILL OPEN DOORS FOR YOU THAT NO ONE CAN SHUT
(REVELATION 3:8, 1 CORINTHIANS 16:8-9)

- God will grant you supernatural favor with the people you need to fulfill His purposes.
- No device or adversary sent from the enemy will be able to stop you.

5. YOUR DREAM WILL GO THROUGH MANY SEASONS BEFORE COMING TO FRUITION
(GALATIANS 6:9, ECCLESIASTES 3:1)

- In the valley of darkness you must walk by faith, not by sight.
- God can take you from the prison to the palace overnight.

6. IT WILL TAKE TEAMWORK TO MAKE THE DREAM WORK
(ECCLESIASTES 4:9-12, LUKE 10:1)

- Only by working with a team will you fulfill the assignment God planted in you.
- Your team must be united because a house divided cannot stand.

7. GOD'S GOT YOUR BACK
(PSALMS 138:7, 2 THESSALONIANS 3:3)

- No weapon formed against you shall prosper.
- <u>Be bold</u> for the Lord is with you wherever you go.

8. YOUR TRUST WILL DETERMINE YOUR LEGACY
(JEREMIAH 17:7-8, GENESIS 26:3-5)

- Focus on the impact you are going to make for the kingdom and not the odds.
- God will not give you a dream unless He plans to bring it into fruition through you.

Self-Assessment Question:
What dream has God planted in you?

Action Steps:
Encourage and strengthen those around you to follow their God given dreams. Find a way to help someone achieve their dream and God will help you achieve yours.

THE 7 STEPS TO OVERCOMING TRIALS AND TRIBULATIONS

Consider it all joy, my brethren, when you encounter various trials, knowing that the testing of your faith produces endurance. And let endurance have its perfect result, so that you may be perfect and complete, lacking in nothing.
James 1:2-4

1. REMEMBER THE GOD YOU SERVE

- Know that God is faithful and that He will NOT fail you. **(1 Corinthians 10:13, Deut. 31:6)**
- Look at the size of your God, not the size of the problem. **(1 Samuel 17:45-47)**
- Plant it down in your spirit that WITH God ALL things are possible. **(Mark 9:20-23)**

2. SEEK HIS PRESENCE DAILY

- Listen to music that ushers in the Holy Spirit. **(Psalms 100:1-5)**
- Stay in His Word and meditate on it constantly. **(Proverbs 4:20-22)**
- Go to your secret place. **(Matthew 6:6)**

3. DEMORIALIZE YOUR ENEMY

- Victory starts with the spoken Word. **(Isaiah 55:10-11, Mark 11:23)**
- Cultivate a spirit of gratitude and praise. **(1 Thessalonians 5:16-18)**
- Intercede for others facing similar challenges. **(Job 42:10)**

4. STAY FOCUSED ON GOD'S PROMISES

- Set your mind on the things of the Spirit. **(Romans 8:5)**
- Adopt the mentality of a conqueror. **(Romans 8:37)**
- Realign your spirit by prayer and fasting. **(Judges 20:26-28, Matthew 17:15-21)**

5. TIGHTEN YOUR INNER CIRCLE

- Remember that iron sharpens iron.
  (Proverbs 17:17, Proverbs 27:17)
- Seek mentors, elders, and wise counsel.
  (Proverbs 20:18, Isaiah 11:2)
- Negative people in your life will prolong the season of struggle.
  (Proverbs 25:19)

6. REFUSE TO CONCEDE

- Look to the cross for hope and strength. **(Romans 12:12)**
- Go to the throne of grace for help. **(Hebrews 4:16)**
- Put God's armor on and keep it on. **(Ephesians 6:10-20)**

7. KEEP YOUR PEACE

- Take it one day at a time. **(Matthew 6:34)**
- Don't make hasty decisions while going through adversity.
  (Proverbs 19:2)
- Surrender completely to your Father. **(James 4:7)**

> **Self-Assessment Question:**
> Am I going to let this season make me angry and bitter, or am I going to let God mold me into someone who is stronger and better?

> **Action Steps:**
> 1. This week seek out people that you know who are facing challenges and sow FAITH, HOPE, and ENCOURAGEMNT into their lives.
> 2. Pray every day this week for the people around you in need.

THE 5 STEPS TO TRUSTING GOD

Trust in the LORD with all thine heart; and lean not unto thine own understanding. In all thy ways acknowledge him, and he shall direct thy paths.
Proverbs 3:5-6

1. UNDERSTAND WHO GOD REALLY IS

- **Elohim** – "The Creator," "God," "God of Might, Power, and Sovereign Authority" **(Genesis 1:1)**
- **El Shaddai** – "The Almighty" **(Genesis 17:1)**
- **Adonai** – "God the Son as sovereign Master". **(Genesis 18:27)**
- **YHWH or Jehovah** – The divine personal name for God. "YHWH" is mentioned over six thousand times in the scriptures. **(Exodus 3:14)**
- **Jehovah-Jireh** – "God the Provider." **(Genesis 22:14)**
- **Jehovah-Rophe** – "God that Heals" **(Exodus 15:26)**
- **Jehovah-Nissi** – "God my Banner, my Victor & Protector," "The Lord Our Banner" **(Exodus 17:15)**
- **Jehovah-Shalom** – "God is Peace" **(Judges 6:24)**
- **Jehovah-Rohi** – "The Lord my shepherd" **(Psalms 23:1)**
- **Jehovah-Shammah** – "The Eternal God; The Lord is There" **(Ezekiel 48:35)**
- **Jehovah-Tsidkenu** – "The Lord Who is our Righteousness" **(2 Corinthians 5:21)**
- **Elah Elahin** – "God of gods" **(Daniel 2:47)**

2. KNOW WHAT THE WORD OF GOD SAYS

- The Word prepares you to succeed in life. **(2 Timothy 3:16, Joshua 1:8)**
- The Word increases your faith. **(Romans 10:17)**

- The Word prevents you from being deceived. **(Acts 17:11)**
- The Word gives wisdom and revelation of the world around you. **(1 John 2:27)**
- The Word helps you defend yourself. **(Ephesians 6:17)**
- The Word guides your steps. **(Psalms 119:105)**
- The Word helps you mature in your walk with God. **(Hebrews 5:12-14)**

3. BELIEVE THAT GOD TRULY LOVES YOU

- God is faithful. **(Jeremiah 31:3, Hebrews 13:5)**
- God gave his son for you. **(John 3:16)**
- You are his treasure. **(Malachi 3:17)**
- He has amazing plans for you. **(Jeremiah 29:11)**
- God cares about what you are going through. **(1 Peter 5:7)**

4. GET ALONE WITH HIM SO YOU CAN HEAR HIM

- This is the way Jesus did it. **(Mark 1:35, Matthew 14:22-23)**
- You gain confidence, rest, and strength in the silence. **(Isaiah 30:15, Mark 6:31)**
- The Lord will reward you when you pray in secret. **(Matthew 6:6)**
- Shutting the noise out helps you get still and put your focus on God. **(Psalms 46:10)**

5. SURRENDER TO HIS WILL

- Humble yourself before him. **(1 Peter 5:6)**
- Bring your body under discipline and crucify the flesh. **(Romans 12:1, Galatians 2:20)**
- You must deny yourself and take up his cross. **(Matthew 16-24-25)**
- You must develop patience. **(Romans 8:25, Psalms 37:7-9)**
- Surrender your every thought to him. **(2 Corinthians 10:5)**

BENEFITS OF TRUSTING THE LORD

1. God will act on your behalf. **(Psalms 37:4-6)**
2. The Lord will give you perfect peace. **(Isaiah 26:3)**
3. He will shield and deliver you in times of trouble. **(Proverbs 30:5, Psalms 91:1-7)**
4. God will make you fruitful in all times, even in the years of drought or famine. **(Jeremiah 17:7-8)**
5. He will give you joy and happiness. **(Proverbs 16:20)**
6. You will prosper. **(Proverbs 28:25-26)**
7. He will grant you the desires of your heart. **(Psalms 37:3-5)**
8. Mercy will surround you. **(Psalms 32:10)**

Self-Assessment Question:
How much do I really trust God? What area of my life do I trust God with the most? In what area of my life do I trust Him the least? What is holding me back from fully trusting Him in that area?

Action Steps:
In the area that you are showing the least amount of trust, read a Bible verse every day on that subject until you surrender completely to him.

THE GOD OF SECOND CHANCES

Then I went down to the potter's house, and there he was, making something on the wheel. But the vessel that he was making of clay was spoiled in the hand of the potter; so he remade it into another vessel, as it pleased the potter to make. Then the word of the LORD came to me saying, "Can I not, O house of Israel, deal with you as this potter does?" declares the LORD. "Behold, like the clay in the potter's hand, so are you in My hand, O house of Israel.
Jeremiah 18:3-6

1. GOD SPECIALIZES IN SECOND CHANCES

- The woman caught in adultery. **(John 8:3-11)**
- David murdered an innocent man. **(2 Samuel 12:13-14)**
- Jonah disobeys God. **(Jonah 2:1-2 & 3:1)**
- Manasseh was a wicked king. **(2 Chronicles 33:10-13)**
- Peter denied Jesus. **(John 21:15-17)**
- King Hezekiah on his deathbed. **(Isaiah 38:1-6)**
- The Prodigal Son **(Luke 15:11-22)**

2. THE FOUR STEPS TO STARTING OVER

- Repent. **(1 John 1:9)**
- Renew your mind with God's Word. **(Romans 12:2)**
- Make amends with those you have offended. **(Matthew 5:23-24)**
- Seek help from pastors, elders, and Christian counselors. **(Proverbs 11:14)**

3. GRACE WILL SET YOU FREE

- No more bondage and no more chains. **(Romans 6:6-7)**
- Your obedience hits the reset button. **(Hebrews 5:9)**
- There's no condemnation in Christ Jesus. **(Romans 8:1)**

4. GOD WILL TURN YOUR MESS INTO A BEAUTIFUL MASTERPIECE

- Humility ushers in restoration. **(James 4:6)**
- What the devil meant for harm, God will make good. **(Genesis 50:20)**
- Your past mistakes will be key to your future victories. **(Romans 8:28)**

5. YOUR BEST DAYS ARE IN FRONT OF YOU

- God's not finished with you yet. **(Isaiah 43:18-21)**
- You will have even greater success the second time around! **(Haggai 2:9)**
- Don't waste the opportunity God is about to bless you with. **(Galatians 6:10)**

6. WHAT DOES GOD SAY ABOUT GIVING OTHERS SECOND CHANCES?

- We are to be patient and compassionate towards others. **(Colossians 3:12-14)**
- Never ask God for something you aren't willing to give someone else. **(Luke 6:36)**
- Show the world what Christ looks like. **(Ephesians 4:31-32)**

7. THE DEVIL IS A LIAR

- Satan will tell you what you have done in the past disqualifies you from grace. **(Ephesians 2:8-9)**
- You don't need to be perfect to go to church, you go to church to praise the one who is. **(Hebrews 4:16)**
- What Jesus did on the cross is much greater than your slipup or backsliding. Return quickly to the Lord, and He will restore you. **(Jeremiah 3:22)**

Self-Assessment Question:
Do you believe God will give you a second chance?

Action Steps:
Give someone in your life a second chance.

PRAYER WARRIOR

1. Remove ALL traces of doubt from your mind.

2. Limit access to anyone who contaminates your faith.

3. Align every aspect of your prayer with God's word.

4. Boldly expect God to honor his promises.

Note: Only those who truly believe will ever experience the power of God!

WHAT THE BIBLE SAYS ABOUT OVERCOMING:
ADDICTION

For freedom Christ has set us free; stand firm therefore, and do not submit again to a yoke of slavery.
Galatians 5:1

No temptation has overtaken you that is not common to man. God is faithful, and he will not let you be tempted beyond your ability, but with the temptation he will also provide the way of escape, that you may be able to endure it.
1 Corinthians 10:13

Be sober-minded; be watchful. Your adversary the devil prowls around like a roaring lion, seeking someone to devour.
1 Peter 5:8

"All things are lawful for me," but not all things are helpful. "All things are lawful for me," but I will not be enslaved by anything.
1 Corinthians 6:12

Wine is a mocker, strong drink a brawler, and whoever is led astray by it is not wise.
Proverbs 20:1

So if the Son sets you free, you will be free indeed.
John 8:36

And do not get drunk with wine, for that is debauchery, but be filled with the Spirit ...
Ephesians 5:18

I can do all things through him who strengthens me.
Philippians 4:13

It is good not to eat meat or drink wine or do anything that causes your brother to stumble.
Romans 14:21

But put on the Lord Jesus Christ, and make no provision for the flesh, to gratify its desires.
Romans 13:14

WHAT THE BIBLE SAYS ABOUT OVERCOMING:
ADULTERY

Thou shalt not commit adultery.
Exodus 20:14

If we confess our sins, he is faithful and just to forgive us our sins and to cleanse us from all unrighteousness.
1 John 1:9

He who commits adultery lacks sense; he who does it destroys himself.
Proverbs 6:32

Let marriage be held in honor among all, and let the marriage bed be undefiled, for God will judge the sexually immoral and adulterous.
Hebrews 13:4

Flee from sexual immorality. Every other sin a person commits is outside the body, but the sexually immoral person sins against his own body.
1 Corinthians 6:18

Everyone who divorces his wife and marries another commits adultery, and he who marries a woman divorced from her husband commits adultery.
Luke 16:18

Husbands, love your wives, even as Christ also loved the church, and gave himself for it; That he might sanctify and cleanse it with the washing of water by the word, that he might present it to himself a glorious church, not having spot, or wrinkle, or any such thing; but that it should be holy and without blemish. So ought men to love their wives as their own bodies. He that loveth his wife loveth himself.
Ephesians 5:25-28

For this is the will of God, your sanctification: that you abstain from sexual immorality; that each one of you know how to control his own body in holiness and honor, not in the passion of lust like the Gentiles who do not know God.
1 Thessalonians 4:3-5

So whoever knows the right thing to do and fails to do it, for him it is sin.
James 4:17

WHAT THE BIBLE SAYS ABOUT OVERCOMING:
ADVERSITY

Count it all joy, my brothers, when you meet trials of various kinds, for you know that the testing of your faith produces steadfastness. And let steadfastness have its full effect, that you may be perfect and complete, lacking in nothing.
James 1:2-4

And we know that for those who love God all things work together for good, for those who are called according to his purpose.
Romans 8:28

He will wipe away every tear from their eyes, and death shall be no more, neither shall there be mourning, nor crying, nor pain anymore, for the former things have passed away.
Revelation 21:4

Beloved, do not be surprised at the fiery trial when it comes upon you to test you, as though something strange were happening to you. But rejoice insofar as you share Christ's sufferings, that you may also rejoice and be glad when his glory is revealed.
1 Peter 4:12-13

Many are the afflictions of the righteous, but the LORD delivers him out of them all.
Psalms 34:19

Blessed is the man who remains steadfast under trial, for when he has stood the test he will receive the crown of life, which God has promised to those who love him.
James 1:12

Who comforts us in all our affliction, so that we may be able to comfort those who are in any affliction, with the comfort with which we ourselves are comforted by God.
2 Corinthians 1:4

Therefore, since we have been justified by faith, we have peace with God through our Lord Jesus Christ. Through him we have also obtained access by faith into this grace in which we stand, and we rejoice in hope of the glory of God. More than that, we rejoice in our sufferings, knowing that suffering produces endurance, and endurance produces character, and character produces hope, and hope does not put us to shame, because God's love has been poured into our hearts through the Holy Spirit who has been given to us.
Romans 5:1-5

WHAT THE BIBLE SAYS ABOUT OVERCOMING:
ANGER

Let all bitterness and wrath and anger and clamor and slander be put away from you, along with all malice.
Ephesians 4:31

Whoever is slow to anger has great understanding, but he who has a hasty temper exalts folly.
Proverbs 14:29

My dear brothers and sisters, take note of this: Everyone should be quick to listen, slow to speak and slow to become angry, because human anger does not produce the righteousness that God desires.
James 1:19-20

A soft answer turns away wrath, but a harsh word stirs up anger.
Proverbs 15:1

Good sense makes one slow to anger, and it is his glory to overlook an offense.
Proverbs 19:11

Be not quick in your spirit to become angry, for anger lodges in the bosom of fools.
Ecclesiastes 7:9

Whoever is slow to anger is better than the mighty, and he who rules his spirit than he who takes a city.
Proverbs 16:32

Be angry and do not sin; do not let the sun go down on your anger, and give no opportunity to the devil.
Ephesians 4:26-27

Beloved, never avenge yourselves, but leave it to the wrath of God, for it is written, "Vengeance is mine, I will repay," says the Lord.
Romans 12:19

Make no friendship with a man given to anger, nor go with a wrathful man, lest you learn his ways and entangle yourself in a snare.
Proverbs 22:24-25

WHAT THE BIBLE SAYS ABOUT OVERCOMING:
BITTERNESS

Strive for peace with everyone, and for the holiness without which no one will see the Lord. See to it that no one fails to obtain the grace of God; that no "root of bitterness" springs up and causes trouble, and by it many become defiled.
Hebrews 12:14-15

Let all bitterness and wrath and anger and clamor and slander be put away from you, along with all malice.
Ephesians 4:31

And whenever you stand praying, forgive, if you have anything against anyone, so that your Father also who is in heaven may forgive you your trespasses.
Mark 11:25

For I see that you are in the gall of bitterness and in the bond of iniquity.
Acts 8:23

Whoever says he is in the light and hates his brother is still in darkness. Whoever loves his brother abides in the light, and in him there is no cause for stumbling. But whoever hates his brother is in the darkness and walks in the darkness, and does not know where he is going, because the darkness has blinded his eyes.
1 John 2:9-11

Pay attention to yourselves! If your brother sins, rebuke him, and if he repents, forgive him, and if he sins against you seven times in the day, and turns to you seven times, saying, 'I repent,' you must forgive him.
Luke 17:3-4

Blessed are the meek, for they shall inherit the earth. "Blessed are those who hunger and thirst for righteousness, for they shall be satisfied." "Blessed are the merciful, for they shall receive mercy." "Blessed are the pure in heart, for they shall see God." "Blessed are the peacemakers, for they shall be called sons of God."
Matthew 5:5-9

WHAT THE BIBLE SAYS ABOUT OVERCOMING:
CANCER/DISEASE

For I will restore health to you, and your wounds I will heal, declares the LORD, because they have called you an outcast: 'It is Zion, for whom no one cares!'
Jeremiah 30:17

He sent out his word and healed them, and delivered them from their destruction.
Psalms 107:20

My son, be attentive to my words; incline your ear to my sayings. Let them not escape from your sight; keep them within your heart. For they are life to those who find them, and healing to all their flesh.
Proverbs 4:20-22

Of David. Bless the LORD, O my soul, and all that is within me, bless his holy name! Bless the LORD, O my soul, and forget not all his benefits, who forgives all your iniquity, who heals all your diseases, who redeems your life from the pit, who crowns you with steadfast love and mercy[.]
Psalms 103:1-4

Have I not commanded you? Be strong and courageous. Do not be frightened, and do not be dismayed, for the LORD your God is with you wherever you go."
Joshua 1:9

But they who wait for the LORD shall renew their strength; they shall mount up with wings like eagles; they shall run and not be weary; they shall walk and not faint.
Isaiah 40:31

And the prayer of faith will save the one who is sick, and the Lord will raise him up. And if he has committed sins, he will be forgiven.
James 5:15

Behold, I will bring to it health and healing, and I will heal them and reveal to them abundance of prosperity and security.
Jeremiah 33:6

He himself bore our sins in his body on the tree, that we might die to sin and live to righteousness. By his wounds you have been healed.
1 Peter 2:24

WHAT THE BIBLE SAYS ABOUT OVERCOMING:
DEPRESSION

When the righteous cry for help, the LORD hears and delivers them out of all their troubles. The LORD is near to the brokenhearted and saves the crushed in spirit.
Psalms 34:17-18

Come to me, all who labor and are heavy laden, and I will give you rest.
Matthew 11:28

Even though I walk through the valley of the shadow of death, I will fear no evil, for you are with me; your rod and your staff, they comfort me.
Psalms 23:4

But they who wait for the LORD shall renew their strength; they shall mount up with wings like eagles; they shall run and not be weary; they shall walk and not faint.
Isaiah 40:31

You have turned for me my mourning into dancing; you have loosed my sackcloth and
clothed me with gladness[.]
Psalms 30:11

I will not leave you as orphans; I will come to you.
John 14:18

To the choirmaster. A Psalms of David. I waited patiently for the LORD; he inclined to me and heard my cry. He drew me up from the pit of destruction, out of the miry bog, and set my feet upon a rock, making my steps secure. He put a new song in my mouth, a song of praise to our God. Many will see and fear, and put their trust in the LORD.
Psalms 40:1-3

I have said these things to you, that in me you may have peace. In the world you will have tribulation. But take heart; I have overcome the world.
John 16:33

For which I am suffering, bound with chains as a criminal. But the word of God is not bound!
2 Timothy 2:9

WHAT THE BIBLE SAYS ABOUT OVERCOMING:
FEAR/ANXIETY

For God hath not given us the spirit of fear; but of power, and of love, and of a sound mind.
2 Timothy 1:7

For I the LORD thy God will hold thy right hand, saying unto thee, Fear not; I will help thee. Isaiah 41:13

I sought the LORD, and he answered me and delivered me from all my fears.
Psalms 34:4

Do not be anxious about anything, but in everything by prayer and supplication with thanksgiving let your requests be made known to God.
Philippians 4:6

When I am afraid, I put my trust in you. In God, whose word I praise, in God I trust; I shall not be afraid. What can flesh do to me?
Psalms 56:3-4

For you did not receive the spirit of slavery to fall back into fear, but you have received the Spirit of adoption as sons, by whom we cry, "Abba! Father!"
Romans 8:15

You shall not be in dread of them, for the LORD your God is in your midst, a great and awesome God.
Deuteronomy 7:21

When I am afraid, I put my trust in you.
Psalms 56:3

Casting all your anxieties on him, because he cares for you.
1 Peter 5:7

He is not afraid of bad news; his heart is firm, trusting in the LORD. His heart is steady; he will not be afraid, until he looks in triumph on his adversaries.
Psalms 112:7-8

WHAT THE BIBLE SAYS ABOUT OVERCOMING:
FINANCIAL DEBT

The LORD will open to you his good treasury, the heavens, to give the rain to your land in its season and to bless all the work of your hands. And you shall lend to many nations, but you shall not borrow.
Deuteronomy 28:12

The rich rules over the poor, and the borrower is the slave of the lender.
Proverbs 22:7

For which of you, desiring to build a tower, does not first sit down and count the cost, whether he has enough to complete it?
Luke 14:28

If then you have not been faithful in the unrighteous wealth, who will entrust to you the true riches?
Luke 16:11

Be not one of those who give pledges, who put up security for debts.
Proverbs 22:26

Owe no one anything, except to love each other, for the one who loves another has fulfilled the law.
Romans 13:8

The wicked borroweth, and payeth not again: but the righteous sheweth mercy, and giveth.
Psalms 37:21

But seek first the kingdom of God and his righteousness, and all these things will be added to you.
Matthew 6:33

He that is faithful in that which is least is faithful also in much: and he that is unjust in the least is unjust also in much.
Luke 16:10

WHAT THE BIBLE SAYS ABOUT OVERCOMING:
JEALOUSY

But if you have bitter jealousy and selfish ambition in your hearts, do not boast and be false to the truth. This is not the wisdom that comes down from above, but is earthly, unspiritual, demonic. For where jealousy and selfish ambition exist, there will be disorder and every vile practice.
James 3:14-16

Do nothing from rivalry or conceit, but in humility count others more significant than yourselves.
Philippians 2:3

Now the works of the flesh are evident: sexual immorality, impurity, sensuality, idolatry, sorcery, enmity, strife, jealousy, fits of anger, rivalries, dissensions, divisions, envy, drunkenness, orgies, and things like these. I warn you, as I warned you before, that those who do such things will not inherit the kingdom of God.
Galatians 5:19-21

For you are still of the flesh. For while there is jealousy and strife among you, are you not of the flesh and behaving only in a human way?
1 Corinthians 3:3

Let us walk properly as in the daytime, not in orgies and drunkenness, not in sexual immorality and sensuality, not in quarreling and jealousy.
Romans 13:13

Love is patient and kind; love does not envy or boast; it is not arrogant or rude. It does not insist on its own way; it is not irritable or resentful; it does not rejoice at wrongdoing,
but rejoices with the truth.
1 Corinthians 13:4-6

So put away all malice and all deceit and hypocrisy and envy and all slander.
1 Peter 2:1

Let us not become conceited, provoking one another, envying one another.
Galatians 5:26

WHAT THE BIBLE SAYS ABOUT OVERCOMING:
LONELINESS

As I was with Moses, so I will be with you; I will never leave you nor forsake you.
Joshua 1:5

At my first defense no one came to stand by me, but all deserted me. May it not be charged against them! But the Lord stood by me and strengthened me, so that through me the message might be fully proclaimed and all the Gentiles might hear it. So I was rescued from the lion's mouth. The Lord will rescue me from every evil deed and bring me safely into his heavenly kingdom. To him be the glory forever and ever. Amen.
2 Timothy 4:16-18

I will not leave you as orphans; I will come to you.
John 14:18

"For I know the plans I have for you," declares the LORD, "plans to prosper you and not to harm you, plans to give you hope and a future."
Jeremiah 29:11

For my father and my mother have forsaken me, but the Lord will take me in.
Psalms 27:10

Turn to me and be gracious to me, for I am lonely and afflicted.
Psalms 25:16

The Lord is near to all who call on him, to all who call on him in truth.
Psalms 145:18

For God alone, O my soul, wait in silence, for my hope is from him.
Psalms 62:5

Father of the fatherless and protector of widows is God in his holy habitation. God settles the solitary in a home; he leads out the prisoners to prosperity, but the rebellious dwell in a parched land.
Psalms 68:5-6

WHAT THE BIBLE SAYS ABOUT OVERCOMING:
LUST

Give not thy strength unto women, nor thy ways to that which destroyeth kings.
Proverbs 31:3

But I say, walk by the Spirit, and you will not gratify the desires of the flesh.
Galatians 5:16

For all that is in the world—the desires of the flesh and the desires of the eyes and pride in possessions—is not from the Father but is from the world.
1 John 2:16

Put to death therefore what is earthly in you: sexual immorality, impurity, passion, evil desire, and covetousness, which is idolatry.
Colossians 3:5

So flee youthful passions and pursue righteousness, faith, love, and peace, along with those who call on the Lord from a pure heart.
2 Timothy 2:22

The body is not meant for sexual immorality, but for the Lord, and the Lord for the body.
1 Corinthians 6:13

Beloved, I urge you as sojourners and exiles to abstain from the passions of the flesh, which wage war against your soul.
1 Peter 2:11

I have made a covenant with my eyes; how then could I gaze at a virgin?
Job 31:1

Let marriage be held in honor among all, and let the marriage bed be undefiled, for God will judge the sexually immoral and adulterous.
Hebrews 13:4

Or do you not know that the unrighteous will not inherit the kingdom of God? Do not be deceived: neither the sexually immoral, nor idolaters, nor adulterers, nor men who practice homosexuality[.]
1 Corinthians 6:9

WHAT THE BIBLE SAYS ABOUT OVERCOMING:
OBESITY

Or do you not know that your body is a temple of the Holy Spirit within you, whom you have from God? You are not your own, for you were bought with a price. So glorify God in your body.
1 Corinthians 6:19-20

Their end is destruction, their god is their belly, and they glory in their shame, with minds set on earthly things.
Philippians 3:19

Beloved, I pray that all may go well with you and that you may be in good health, as it goes well with your soul.
3 John 1:2

But the fruit of the Spirit is love, joy, peace, patience, kindness, goodness, faithfulness, gentleness, self-control; against such things there is no law. And those who belong to Christ Jesus have crucified the flesh with its passions and desires.
Galatians 5:22-24

Be not among drunkards or among gluttonous eaters of meat, for the drunkard and the glutton will come to poverty, and slumber will clothe them with rags.
Proverbs 23:20-21

But watch yourselves lest your hearts be weighed down with dissipation and drunkenness and cares of this life, and that day come upon you suddenly like a trap.
Luke 21:34

Come, everyone who thirsts, come to the waters; and he who has no money, come, buy and eat! Come, buy wine and milk without money and without price. Why do you spend your money for that which is not bread, and your labor for that which does not satisfy? Listen diligently to me, and eat what is good, and delight yourselves in rich food.
Isaiah 55:1-2

He who keeps the law is a discerning son, but he who is a companion of gluttons humiliates his father.
Proverbs 28:7

WHAT THE BIBLE SAYS ABOUT OVERCOMING:
PAIN AND SUFFERERING

He will wipe away every tear from their eyes, and death shall be no more, neither shall there be mourning, nor crying, nor pain anymore, for the former things have passed away.
Revelation 21:4

Beloved, do not be surprised at the fiery trial when it comes upon you to test you, as though something strange were happening to you. But rejoice insofar as you share Christ's sufferings, that you may also rejoice and be glad when his glory is revealed.
1 Peter 4:12-13

"For I know the plans I have for you," declares the LORD, "plans to prosper you and not to harm you, plans to give you hope and a future."
Jeremiah 29:11

More than that, we rejoice in our sufferings, knowing that suffering produces endurance, and endurance produces character, and character produces hope, and hope does not put us to shame, because God's love has been poured into our hearts through the Holy Spirit
who has been given to us.
Romans 5:3-5

Count it all joy, my brothers, when you meet trials of various kinds, for you know that the testing of your faith produces steadfastness. And let steadfastness have its full effect, that you may be perfect and complete, lacking in nothing.
James 1:2-4

I have said these things to you, that in me you may have peace. In the world you will have tribulation. But take heart; I have overcome the world.
John 16:33

Is anyone among you sick? Let him call for the elders of the church, and let them pray over him, anointing him with oil in the name of the Lord. And the prayer of faith will save the one who is sick, and the Lord will raise him up. And if he has committed sins, he will be forgiven. Therefore, confess your sins to one another and pray for one another, that you may be healed. The prayer of a righteous person has great power as it is working.
James 5:14-16

WHAT THE BIBLE SAYS ABOUT OVERCOMING:
IMPATIENCE

And let us not grow weary of doing good, for in due season we will reap, if we do not give up.
Galatians 6:9

Rejoice in hope, be patient in tribulation, be constant in prayer.
Romans 12:12

Be still before the LORD and wait patiently for him; fret not yourself over the one who prospers in his way, over the man who carries out evil devices! Refrain from anger, and forsake wrath! Fret not yourself; it tends only to evil. For the evildoers shall be cut off, but those who wait for the LORD shall inherit the land.
Psalms 37:7-9

And thus Abraham, having patiently waited, obtained the promise.
Hebrews 6:15

Do not be anxious about anything, but in everything by prayer and supplication with thanksgiving let your requests be made known to God.
Philippians 4:6

But let patience have her perfect work, that ye may be perfect and entire, wanting nothing.
James 1:4

The Lord is not slow to fulfill his promise as some count slowness, but is patient toward you, not wishing that any should perish, but that all should reach repentance.
2 Peter 3:9

As for that in the good soil, they are those who, hearing the word, hold it fast in an honest and good heart, and bear fruit with patience.
Luke 8:15

So that you may not be sluggish, but imitators of those who through faith and patience inherit the promises.
Hebrews 6:12

WHAT THE BIBLE SAYS ABOUT OVERCOMING:
PRIDE

Pride goes before destruction, a haughty spirit before a fall.
Proverbs 16:18

For if anyone thinks he is something, when he is nothing, he deceives himself.
Galatians 6:3

Let another praise you, and not your own mouth; a stranger, and not your own lips.
Proverbs 27:2

But he gives more grace. Therefore it says, "God opposes the proud,
but gives grace to the humble."
James 4:6

The fear of the LORD is hatred of evil. Pride and arrogance and the way of evil
and perverted speech I hate.
Proverbs 8:13

For men will be lovers of themselves, lovers of money, boasters, proud, blasphemers, disobedient to parents, unthankful, unholy, unloving, unforgiving, slanderers, without self-control, brutal, despisers of good, traitors, headstrong, haughty, lovers of pleasure rather than lovers of God, having a form of godliness but denying its power. And from such people turn away!
2 Timothy 3:2-5

Not that we dare to classify or compare ourselves with some of those who are commending themselves. But when they measure themselves by one another and compare themselves with one another, they are without understanding.
2 Corinthians 10:12

Do not love the world or the things in the world. If anyone loves the world, the love of the Father is not in him. For all that is in the world—the desires of the flesh and the desires of the eyes and pride in possessions—is not from the Father but is from the world. And the world is passing away along with its desires, but whoever does the will of God abides forever.
1 John 2:15-17

WHAT THE BIBLE SAYS ABOUT OVERCOMING:
STRESS

Cast your burden on the LORD, and he will sustain you;
he will never permit the righteous to be moved.
Psalms 55:22

Peace I leave with you; my peace I give to you. Not as the world gives do I give to you. Let not your hearts be troubled, neither let them be afraid.
John 14:27

Do not be anxious about anything, but in everything by prayer and supplication with thanksgiving let your requests be made known to God.
Philippians 4:6

Come to me, all who labor and are heavy laden, and I will give you rest. Take my yoke upon you, and learn from me, for I am gentle and lowly in heart, and you will find rest for your souls. For my yoke is easy, and my burden is light.
Matthew 11:28-30

And which of you by being anxious can add a single hour to his span of life?
Matthew 6:27

Therefore do not be anxious about tomorrow, for tomorrow will be anxious for itself. Sufficient for the day is its own trouble.
Matthew 6:34

The LORD will fight for you; you need only to be still.
Exodus 14:14

I can do all things through him who strengthens me.
Philippians 4:13

For God hath not given us the spirit of fear; but of power, and of love, and of a sound mind.
2 Timothy 1:7

Then Jesus said to his disciples: "Therefore I tell you, do not worry about your life, what you will eat; or about your body, what you will wear.
Luke 12:22

BLESSED AND UNSTOPPABLE

ALIGNING WITH THE BLESSING

THE COVENANT BLESSING

This is the covenant blessing God made to Abraham and his descendants mentioned in Deuteronomy 28:1-14.

And it shall come to pass, if thou shalt hearken diligently unto the voice of the LORD thy God, to observe and to do all his commandments which I command thee this day, that the LORD thy God will set thee on high above all nations of the earth: And all these blessings shall come on thee, and overtake thee, if thou shalt hearken unto the voice of the LORD thy God.

Blessed shalt thou be in the city, and blessed shalt thou be in the field.

Blessed shall be the fruit of thy body, and the fruit of thy ground, and the fruit of thy cattle, the increase of thy kine, and the flocks of thy sheep.

Blessed shall be thy basket and thy store.

Blessed shalt thou be when thou comest in, and blessed shalt thou be when thou goest out.

The LORD shall cause thine enemies that rise up against thee to be smitten before thy face: they shall come out against thee one way, and flee before thee seven ways. The LORD shall command the blessing upon thee in thy storehouses, and in all that thou settest thine hand unto; and he shall bless thee in the land which the LORD thy God giveth thee. The LORD shall establish thee an holy people unto himself, as he hath sworn unto thee, if thou shalt keep the commandments of the LORD thy God, and walk in his ways. And all people of the earth shall see that thou art called by the name of the LORD; and they shall be afraid of thee. And the

LORD shall make thee plenteous in goods, in the fruit of thy body, and in the fruit of thy cattle, and in the fruit of thy ground, in the land which the LORD sware unto thy fathers to give thee. The LORD shall open unto thee his good treasure, the heaven to give the rain unto thy land in his season, and to bless all the work of thine hand: and thou shalt lend unto many nations, and thou shalt not borrow. And the LORD shall make thee the head, and not the tail; and thou shalt be above only, and thou shalt not be beneath; if that thou hearken unto the commandments of the LORD thy God, which I command thee this day, to observe and to do them: And thou shalt not go aside from any of the words which I command thee this day, to the right hand, or to the left, to go after other gods to serve them.

UNDERSTANDING THE COVENANT

As sinners by nature, we alone are unable to fulfill the requirements needed to receive this blessing. There is no action or thing that we could ever do, as born sinners, to deserve it. To graft us back into the kingdom, Christ freely offers His righteousness to us, so that we can offer it up to God as obedience. Our faith in Christ makes us heirs to the promise and as heirs we can now claim for our own lives full possession of every single gift promised in this covenant. It is only by God's Grace and His righteousness that we have any legal right to it. This powerful verse from the New Testament confirms this:

> *If you belong to Christ, then you are Abraham's seed, and heirs according to the promise.*
> Galatians 3:29

In order to walk in the fullness of the blessing, we must effectively align ourselves with God's word and principles that dictate access to it. By applying his wisdom to our lives, we are able to draw out and experience the overflowing abundance of His promise.

HOW TO TAKE THE LIMITS OFF OF GOD

Yea, they turned back and tempted God, and limited the Holy One of Israel. They remembered not his hand, nor the day when he delivered them from the enemy.
Psalms 78:41-42

1. UNDERSTAND THE GOD YOU ARE APPROACHING

- He is above all, over all, and controls all. **(Deuteronomy 10:17, 1 Chronicles 29:11)**
- There is no limit to his might, wonders, or glory. **(Jude 1:25)**
- The power and authority of His word is limitless. **(Ephesians 1:19, Psalms 147:5)**

2. AWAKEN TO THE POWER WITHIN YOU

- The Holy Spirit is real power! **(Ephesians 3:16, 2 Corinthians 3:17)**
- The same spirit that produced the miracles of the Bible is in you. **(1 Corinthians 3:16, 2 Corinthians 13:5, Acts 10:34-35 &38)**
- Whatever you need His grace is sufficient. **(2 Corinthians 9:8, Philippians 4:13)**

3. REMEMBER THE AWESOME MIRACLES GOD PERFORMED FOR HIS PEOPLE

- The Apostles performed many miracles of healing. **(Acts 5:12-16)**
- God blessed Isaac with wealth and riches. **(Genesis 26:12-13)**
- God delivered his servants from the fire. **(Daniel 3:19-28)**

4. CHANGE YOUR PERCEPTION OF HIM

- Believe God is bigger than your circumstances. **(Jeremiah 32:27)**
- Understand that He really loves you. **(Romans 8:35-39)**
- Discover your true identity in Christ. **(1 Peter 2:9)**

5. GO ALL IN (STEP OUT IN FAITH)

- Take him at His word. **(Numbers 23:19)**
- Trust Him to do the impossible. **(Matthew 19:26, Luke 1:37)**
- Walk the word out with no compromise. **(1 Kings 18:21)**

6. TAKE THE LIMITS OFF YOUR PRAYERS, WORSHIP, AND PRAISE

- God deserves awesome praise. **(Revelation 4:11)**
- All the mighty men of faith in the bible majored in these three. **(Daniel 6:10)**
- It breaks the yoke of bondage. **(Acts 16:25-26)**

7. RAISE YOUR EXPECTATIONS OF HIM

- Know that He can do way more than you could ever imagine. **(Ephesians 3:20)**
- Pray BOLD stop the sun type prayers and trust him to do it. **(Joshua 10:12-13)**
- Believe He will massively multiply His kingdom through you. **(Acts 2:40-43 & 46-47)**

Self-Assessment Question:
In what areas of my life am I limiting God?

Action Steps:
God has an amazing future planned for you. All you have to do is take Him out of that limited box you have Him in. This week step out in faith, start asking BIG, dreaming BIG, and believing BIG, and you will be amazed at how God starts to move in your life!

THE TWELVE ENEMIES

NO VISION
DOUBT
FEAR
PRIDE
LUST
IGNORANCE
COMPLACENCY
UNFORGIVENESS
NO WISE COUNSEL
A NEGATIVE INNER CIRCLE
LACK OF SELF-DISCIPLINE
NO SELF-AWARENESS

THE 12 ENEMIES OF GREATNESS

WHAT THE BIBLE SAYS ABOUT:
ABUNDANCE

Now unto him that is able to do exceeding abundantly above all that we ask or think, according to the power that worketh in us...
Ephesians 3:20

And my God will supply every need of yours according to his riches in glory in Christ Jesus. Philippians 4:19

The thief comes only to steal and kill and destroy. I came that they may have life and have it abundantly.
John 10:10

May the LORD, the God of your ancestors, increase you a thousand times and bless you as he has promised!
Deuteronomy 1:11

The LORD will open to you his good treasury, the heavens, to give the rain to your land in its season and to bless all the work of your hands. And you shall lend to many nations, but you shall not borrow.
Deuteronomy 28:12

And God is able to make all grace abound to you, so that having all sufficiency in all things at all times, you may abound in every good work.
2 Corinthians 9:8

He said to them, "Cast the net on the right side of the boat, and you will find some." So they cast it, and now they were not able to haul it in, because of the quantity of fish.
John 21:6

The LORD knows the days of the blameless, and their heritage will remain forever; they are not put to shame in evil times; in the days of famine they have abundance.
Psalms 37:18-19

When Isaac planted his crops that year, he harvested a hundred times more grain than he planted, for the LORD blessed him. He became a very rich man, and his wealth continued to grow.
Genesis 26:12-13

WHAT THE BIBLE SAYS ABOUT:
BOLDNESS

The wicked flee when no one pursues, but the righteous are bold as a lion.
Proverbs 28:1

And when they had prayed, the place in which they were gathered together was shaken, and they were all filled with the Holy Spirit and continued to speak the word of God with boldness.
Acts 4:31

Now when they saw the boldness of Peter and John, and perceived that they were uneducated, common men, they were astonished. And they recognized that they had been with Jesus.
Acts 4:13

Have I not commanded you? Be strong and courageous. Do not be frightened, and do not be dismayed, for the LORD your God is with you wherever you go.
Joshua 1:9

But though we had already suffered and been shamefully treated at Philippi, as you know, we had boldness in our God to declare to you the gospel of God in the midst of much conflict.
1 Thessalonians 2:2

Let us therefore come boldly to the throne of grace, that we may obtain mercy, and find grace to help in time of need.
Hebrews 4:16

Be strong and courageous. Do not fear or be in dread of them, for it is the LORD your God who goes with you. He will not leave you or forsake you.
Deuteronomy 31:6

But Caleb quieted the people before Moses and said, "Let us go up at once and occupy it, for we are well able to overcome it.
Numbers 13:30

No weapon that is fashioned against you shall succeed, and you shall confute every tongue that rises against you in judgment. This is the heritage of the servants of the LORD and their vindication from me, declares the LORD.
Isaiah 54:17

WHAT THE BIBLE SAYS ABOUT:
FAITH

And without faith it is impossible to please him, for whoever would draw near to God must believe that he exists and that he rewards those who seek him.
Hebrews 11:6

And Jesus answered them, "Have faith in God. Truly, I say to you, whoever says to this mountain, 'Be taken up and thrown into the sea,' and does not doubt in his heart, but believes that what he says will come to pass, it will be done for him. Therefore I tell you, whatever you ask in prayer, believe that you have received it, and it will be yours."
Mark 11:22-24

And all things, whatsoever ye shall ask in prayer, believing, ye shall receive.
Matthew 21:22

Now faith is the assurance of things hoped for, the conviction of things not seen.
Hebrews 11:1

For we walk by faith, not by sight.
2 Corinthians 5:7

If any of you lacks wisdom, let him ask God, who gives generously to all without reproach, and it will be given him. But let him ask in faith, with no doubting, for the one who doubts is like a wave of the sea that is driven and tossed by the wind. For that person must not suppose that he will receive anything from the Lord; he is a double-minded man, unstable in all his ways.
James 1:5-8

Yet we know that a person is not justified by works of the law but through faith in Jesus Christ, so we also have believed in Christ Jesus, in order to be justified by faith in Christ and not by works of the law, because by works of the law no one will be justified.
Galatians 2:16

No distrust made him waver concerning the promise of God, but he grew strong in his faith as he gave glory to God, fully convinced that God was able to do what he had promised.
Romans 4:20-21

WHAT THE BIBLE SAYS ABOUT:
FAMILY

But if anyone does not provide for his relatives, and especially for members of his household, he has denied the faith and is worse than an unbeliever.
1 Timothy 5:8

Honor your father and your mother, that your days may be long in the land that the LORD your God is giving you.
Exodus 20:12

Train up a child in the way he should go; even when he is old he will not depart from it.
Proverbs 22:6

Your offspring shall be like the dust of the earth, and you shall spread abroad to the west and to the east and to the north and to the south, and in you and your offspring shall all the families of the earth be blessed.
Genesis 28:14

Children, obey your parents in the Lord, for this is right. "Honor your father and mother" (this is the first commandment with a promise).
Ephesians 6:1-2

My son, keep your father's command and do not forsake your mother's teaching.
Proverbs: 6:20

But if serving the LORD seems undesirable to you, then choose for yourselves this day whom you will serve, whether the gods your ancestors served beyond the Euphrates, or the gods of the Amorites, in whose land you are living. But as for me and my household, we will serve the LORD.
Joshua 24:15

For if someone does not know how to manage his own household, how will he care for God's church?
1 Timothy 3:5

WHAT THE BIBLE SAYS ABOUT:
FORGIVENESS

And whenever you stand praying, forgive, if you have anything against anyone, so that your Father also who is in heaven may forgive you your trespasses.
Mark 11:25

But if you do not forgive others their trespasses, neither will your Father forgive your trespasses.
Matthew 6:15

Be kind to one another, tenderhearted, forgiving one another, as God in Christ forgave you.
Ephesians 4:32

If we confess our sins, he is faithful and just to forgive us our sins and to cleanse us from all unrighteousness.
1 John 1:9

Then Peter came up and said to him, "Lord, how often will my brother sin against me, and I forgive him? As many as seven times?" Jesus said to him, "I do not say to you seven times,
but seventy times seven."
Matthew 18:21-22

Judge not, and you will not be judged; condemn not, and you will not be condemned; forgive, and you will be forgiven[.]
Luke 6:37

Repay no one evil for evil, but give thought to do what is honorable in the sight of all.
Romans 12:17

Brothers, if anyone is caught in any transgression, you who are spiritual should restore him in a spirit of gentleness. Keep watch on yourself, lest you too be tempted.
Galatians 6:1

And Jesus said, "Father, forgive them, for they know not what they do."
Luke 23:34

WHAT THE BIBLE SAYS ABOUT:
GRACE

For sin will have no dominion over you, since you are not under law but under grace.
Romans 6:14

But he said to me, "My grace is sufficient for you, for my power is made perfect in weakness." Therefore I will boast all the more gladly of my weaknesses, so that the power of Christ may rest upon me.
2 Corinthians 12:9

For by grace you have been saved through faith. And this is not your own doing; it is the gift of God, not a result of works, so that no one may boast.
Ephesians 2:8-9

Let us then with confidence draw near to the throne of grace, that we may receive mercy and find grace to help in time of need.
Hebrews 4:16

And from his fullness we have all received, grace upon grace.
John 1:16

You then, my child, be strengthened by the grace that is in Christ Jesus…
2 Timothy 2:1

And the Word became flesh and dwelt among us, and we have seen his glory, glory as of the only Son from the Father, full of grace and truth.
John 1:14

What shall we say then? Are we to continue in sin that grace may abound? By no means! How can we who died to sin still live in it? Do you not know that all of us who have been baptized into Christ Jesus were baptized into his death? We were buried therefore with him by baptism into death, in order that, just as Christ was raised from the dead by the glory of the Father, we too might walk in newness of life.
Romans 6:1-4

But as you excel in everything—in faith, in speech, in knowledge, in all earnestness, and in our love for you—see that you excel in this act of grace also.
2 Corinthians 8:7

WHAT THE BIBLE SAYS ABOUT:
GRATITUDE

This is the day that the LORD has made; let us rejoice and be glad in it.
Psalms 118:24

Give thanks in all circumstances; for this is the will of God in Christ Jesus for you.
1 Thessalonians 5:18

And whatever you do, in word or deed, do everything in the name of the Lord Jesus, giving thanks to God the Father through him.
Colossians 3:17

Therefore let us be grateful for receiving a kingdom that cannot be shaken, and thus let us offer to God acceptable worship, with reverence and awe...
Hebrews 12:28

The one who offers thanksgiving as his sacrifice glorifies me; to one who orders his way rightly I will show the salvation of God!
Psalms 50:23

You are my God, and I will give thanks to you; you are my God; I will extol you. Oh give thanks to the LORD, for he is good; for his steadfast love endures forever!
Psalms 118:28-29

Through him then let us continually offer up a sacrifice of praise to God, that is, the fruit of lips that acknowledge his name.
Hebrews 13:15

Oh give thanks to the LORD; call upon his name; make known his deeds among the peoples!
Psalms 105:1

The LORD is my strength and my shield; in him my heart trusts, and I am helped; my heart exults, and with my song I give thanks to him.
Psalms 28:7

Bless the LORD, O my soul, and forget not all his benefits...
Psalms 103:2

WHAT THE BIBLE SAYS ABOUT:
HAPPINESS

As the Father has loved me, so have I loved you. Abide in my love. If you keep my commandments, you will abide in my love, just as I have kept my Father's commandments and abide in his love. These things I have spoken to you, that my joy may be in you, and that your joy may be full.
John 15:9-11

I perceived that there is nothing better for them than to be joyful and to do good as long as they live; also that everyone should eat and drink and take pleasure in all his toil—this is God's gift to man.
Ecclesiastes 3:12-13

Until now you have asked nothing in my name. Ask, and you will receive, that your joy may be full.
John 16:24

Rejoice in the Lord always; again I will say, rejoice.
Philippians 4:4

Not that I am speaking of being in need, for I have learned in whatever situation I am to be content.
Philippians 4:11

Delight yourself in the LORD, and he will give you the desires of your heart.
Psalms 37:4

With joy you will draw water from the wells of salvation.
Isaiah 12:3

Therefore my heart is glad, and my whole being rejoices; my flesh also dwells secure.
Psalms 16:9

A joyful heart is good medicine, but a crushed spirit dries up the bones.
Proverbs 17:22

For he will not much remember the days of his life because God keeps him occupied with joy in his heart.
Ecclesiastes 5:20

WHAT THE BIBLE SAYS ABOUT:
HEALING

Is anyone among you sick? Let him call for the elders of the church, and let them pray over him, anointing him with oil in the name of the Lord.
James 5:14

Therefore, confess your sins to one another and pray for one another, that you may be healed. The prayer of a righteous person has great power as it is working.
James 5:16

But he was pierced for our transgressions, he was crushed for our iniquities; the punishment that brought us peace was on him, and by his wounds we are healed.
Isaiah 53:5

And he called to him his twelve disciples and gave them authority over unclean spirits, to cast them out, and to heal every disease and every affliction.
Matthew 10:1

No weapon that is formed against thee shall prosper; and every tongue that shall rise against thee in judgment thou shalt condemn. This is the heritage of the servants of the LORD, and their righteousness is of me, saith the LORD.
Isaiah 54:17

For I will restore health unto thee, and I will heal thee of thy wounds, saith the LORD;
Jeremiah 30:17

I have seen his ways, but I will heal him; I will lead him and restore comfort to him and his mourners, creating the fruit of the lips. Peace, peace, to the far and to the near," says the LORD, "and I will heal him.
Isaiah 57:18-19

The LORD sustains him on his sickbed; in his illness you restore him to full health.
Psalms 41:3

WHAT THE BIBLE SAYS ABOUT:
HEALTH

Or do you not know that your body is a temple of the Holy Spirit within you, whom you have from God? You are not your own, for you were bought with a price. So glorify God in your body.
1 Corinthians 6:19-20

So, whether you eat or drink, or whatever you do, do all to the glory of God.
1 Corinthians 10:31

With a long life I will satisfy him And let him see My salvation.
Psalms 91:16

My son, attend to my words; incline thine ear unto my sayings. Let them not depart from thine eyes; keep them in the midst of thine heart. For they are life unto those that find them, and health to all their flesh.
Proverbs 4:20-22

You shall work six days, but on the seventh day you shall rest; even during plowing time and harvest you shall rest.
Exodus 34:21

Beloved, I wish above all things that thou mayest prosper and be in health, even as thy soul prospereth.
3 John 1:2

Pleasant words are as a honeycomb, sweet to the soul, and health to the bones.
Proverbs 16:24

After all, no one ever hated their own body, but they feed and care for their body, just as Christ does the church.
Ephesians 5:29

I urge you, brothers, in view of God's mercy, to offer your bodies as living sacrifices, holy and pleasing to God – this is your spiritual act of worship.
Romans 12:1

WHAT THE BIBLE SAYS ABOUT:
HOPE

"For I know the plans I have for you," declares the LORD, "plans to prosper you and not to harm you, plans to give you hope and a future."
Jeremiah 29:11

Return to your stronghold, O prisoners of hope; today I declare that I will restore to you double.
Zechariah 9:12

And now, O Lord, for what do I wait? My hope is in you.
Psalms 39:7

Surely there is a future, and your hope will not be cut off.
Proverbs 23:18

The hope of the righteous brings joy, but the expectation of the wicked will perish.
Proverbs 10:28

But I will hope continually and will praise you yet more and more.
Psalms 71:14

"The LORD is my portion," says my soul, "therefore I will hope in him."
Lamentations 3:24

Since we have such a hope, we are very bold....
2 Corinthians 3:12

Uphold me according to your promise, that I may live,
and let me not be put to shame in my hope!
Psalms 119:116

May the God of hope fill you with all joy and peace in believing, so that by the power of
the Holy Spirit you may abound in hope.
Romans 15:13

WHAT THE BIBLE SAYS ABOUT:
INVESTING

Let Pharaoh appoint commissioners over the land to take a fifth of the harvest of Egypt during the seven years of abundance. They should collect all the food of these good years that are coming and store up the grain under the authority of Pharaoh, to be kept in the cities for food. This food should be held in reserve for the country, to be used during the seven years of famine that will come upon Egypt, so that the country may not be ruined by the famine.
Genesis 41:34-36

The point is this: whoever sows sparingly will also reap sparingly, and whoever sows bountifully will also reap bountifully.
2 Corinthians 9:6

Dishonest money dwindles away, but he who gathers money little by little makes it grow.
Proverbs 13:11

"Bring the full tithe into the storehouse, that there may be food in my house. And thereby put me to the test," says the LORD of hosts, "if I will not open the windows of heaven for you and pour down for you a blessing until there is no more need."
Malachi 3:10

Cast your bread upon the waters, for you will find it after many days. Give a portion to seven, or even to eight, for you know not what disaster may happen on earth.
Ecclesiastes 11:1-2

He will love you, bless you, and multiply you. He will also bless the fruit of your womb and the fruit of your ground, your grain and your wine and your oil, the increase of your herds and the young of your flock, in the land that he swore to your fathers to give you.
Deuteronomy 7:13

Also it is not good for a person to be without knowledge, and he who hurries his footsteps errs.
Proverbs 19:2

Go to the ant, you sluggard; consider its ways and be wise! It has no commander, no overseer or ruler, yet it stores its provisions in summer and gathers its food at harvest.
Proverbs 6:6-8

The plans of the diligent lead to profit as surely as haste leads to poverty.
Proverbs 21:5

WHAT THE BIBLE SAYS ABOUT:
LEADERSHIP

But Jesus called them to him and said, "You know that the rulers of the Gentiles lord it over them, and their great ones exercise authority over them. It shall not be so among you. But whoever would be great among you must be your servant, and whoever would be first among you must be your slave, even as the Son of Man came not to be served but to serve, and to give his life as a ransom for many."
Matthew 20:25-28

When he had washed their feet and put on his outer garments and resumed his place, he said to them, "Do you understand what I have done to you? You call me Teacher and Lord, and you are right, for so I am. If I then, your Lord and Teacher, have washed your feet, you also ought to wash one another's feet. For I have given you an example,
that you also should do just as I have done to you."
John 13:12-15

The saying is trustworthy: If anyone aspires to the office of overseer, he desires a noble task. Therefore an overseer must be above reproach, the husband of one wife, sober-minded, self-controlled, respectable, hospitable, able to teach, not a drunkard, not violent but gentle, not quarrelsome, not a lover of money. He must manage his own household well, with all dignity keeping his children submissive, for if someone does not know how to manage his own household, how will he care for God's church?
1 Timothy 3:1-7

Moreover, look for able men from all the people, men who fear God, who are trustworthy and hate a bribe, and place such men over the people as chiefs of thousands, of hundreds, of fifties, and of tens.
Exodus 18:21

Not domineering over those in your charge, but being examples to the flock.
1 Peter 5:3

Choose for your tribes wise, understanding, and experienced men,
and I will appoint them as your heads.
Deuteronomy 1:13

And I heard the voice of the Lord saying, "Whom shall I send, and who will go for us?" Then I said, "Here am I! Send me."
Isaiah 6:8

WHAT THE BIBLE SAYS ABOUT:
LOVE

Love is patient and kind; love does not envy or boast; it is not arrogant or rude. It does not insist on its own way; it is not irritable or resentful; it does not rejoice at wrongdoing, but rejoices with the truth. Love bears all things, believes all things, hopes all things, endures all things. Love never ends. As for prophecies, they will pass away; as for tongues, they will cease; as for knowledge, it will pass away.
1 Corinthians 13:4-8

A new commandment I give to you, that you love one another: just as I have loved you, you also are to love one another. By this all people will know that you are my disciples, if you have love for one another.
John 13:34-35

And above all these put on love, which binds everything together in perfect harmony.
Colossians 3:14

There is no fear in love, but perfect love casts out fear. For fear has to do with punishment, and whoever fears has not been perfected in love.
1 John 4:18

"Teacher, which is the great commandment in the Law?" And he said to him, "You shall love the Lord your God with all your heart and with all your soul and with all your mind. This is the great and first commandment. And a second is like it: You shall love your neighbor as yourself. On these two commandments depend all the Law and the Prophets."
Matthew 22:36-40

Let all that you do be done in love.
1 Corinthians 16:14

So now faith, hope, and love abide, these three; but the greatest of these is love.
1 Corinthians 13:13

WHAT THE BIBLE SAYS ABOUT:
MARRIAGE

Therefore a man shall leave his father and his mother and hold fast to his wife, and they shall become one flesh.
Genesis 2:24

Husbands, love your wives, as Christ loved the church and gave himself up for her, that he might sanctify her, having cleansed her by the washing of water with the word, so that he might present the church to himself in splendor, without spot or wrinkle or any such thing, that she might be holy and without blemish. In the same way husbands should love their wives as their own bodies. He who loves his wife loves himself.
Ephesians 5:25-28

Let marriage be held in honor among all, and let the marriage bed be undefiled, for God will judge the sexually immoral and adulterous.
Hebrews 13:4

"'And the two shall become one flesh.' So they are no longer two but one flesh. What therefore God has joined together, let not man separate."
Mark 10:8-9

Do not be unequally yoked with unbelievers. For what partnership has righteousness with lawlessness? Or what fellowship has light with darkness?
2 Corinthians 6:14

Likewise, husbands, live with your wives in an understanding way, showing honor to the woman as the weaker vessel, since they are heirs with you of the grace of life, so that your prayers may not be hindered.
1 Peter 3:7

An excellent wife who can find? She is far more precious than jewels.
Proverbs 31:10

He who finds a wife finds a good thing and obtains favor from the LORD.
Proverbs 18:22

WHAT THE BIBLE SAYS ABOUT:
MINDSET

Do not be conformed to this world, but be transformed by the renewal of your mind, that by testing you may discern what is the will of God, what is good and acceptable and perfect.
Romans 12:2

Set your minds on things that are above, not on things that are on earth.
Colossians 3:2

Finally, brothers, whatever is true, whatever is honorable, whatever is just, whatever is pure, whatever is lovely, whatever is commendable, if there is any excellence, if there is anything worthy of praise, think about these things.
Philippians 4:8

For those who live according to the flesh set their minds on the things of the flesh, but those who live according to the Spirit set their minds on the things of the Spirit. For to set the mind on the flesh is death, but to set the mind on the Spirit is life and peace. For the mind that is set on the flesh is hostile to God, for it does not submit to God's law; indeed, it cannot. Those who are in the flesh cannot please God.
Romans 8:5-8

Casting down imaginations, and every high thing that exalteth itself against the knowledge of God, and bringing into captivity every thought to the obedience of Christ[.]
2 Corinthians 10:5

And the peace of God, which transcends all understanding, will guard your hearts and your minds in Christ Jesus.
Philippians 4:7

For God hath not given us the spirit of fear; but of power, and of love, and of a sound mind.
2 Timothy 1:7

I will meditate on your precepts and fix my eyes on your ways.
Psalms 119:15

Then make my joy complete by being like-minded, having the same love, being one in spirit and of one mind.
Philippians 2:2

WHAT THE BIBLE SAYS ABOUT:
MONEY

But thou shalt remember the LORD thy God: for it is he that giveth thee power to get wealth, that he may establish his covenant which he sware unto thy fathers, as it is this day.
Deuteronomy 8:18

Isaac planted crops in that land and the same year reaped a hundredfold, because the LORD blessed him. The man became rich, and his wealth continued to grow until he became very wealthy.
Genesis 26:12-13

For the love of money is a root of all kinds of evils. It is through this craving that some have wandered away from the faith and pierced themselves with many pangs.
1 Timothy 6:10

The blessing of the LORD makes rich, and he adds no sorrow with it.
Proverbs 10:22

No one can serve two masters, for either he will hate the one and love the other, or he will be devoted to the one and despise the other. You cannot serve God and money.
Matthew 6:24

Lazy hands make for poverty, but diligent hands bring wealth.
Proverbs 10:4

And my God will meet all your needs according to his glorious riches in Christ Jesus.
Philippians 4:19

A good man leaves an inheritance to his children's children, but the sinner's wealth is laid up for the righteous.
Proverbs 13:22

And God will generously provide all you need. Then you will always have everything you need and plenty left over to share with others.
2 Corinthians 9:8

And if you are untrustworthy about worldly wealth, who will trust you with the true riches of heaven?
Luke 16:11

WHAT THE BIBLE SAYS ABOUT:
PRAYER

Do not be anxious about anything, but in everything by prayer and supplication with thanksgiving let your requests be made known to God.
Philippians 4:6

Rejoice always, pray without ceasing, give thanks in all circumstances; for this is the will of God in Christ Jesus for you.
1 Thessalonians 5:16-18

But when you pray, go into your room and shut the door and pray to your Father who is in secret. And your Father who sees in secret will reward you. And when you pray, do not heap up empty phrases as the Gentiles do, for they think that they will be heard for their many words.
Matthew 6:6-7

When the righteous cry for help, the LORD hears and delivers them out of all their troubles.
Psalms 34:17

Then you will call upon me and come and pray to me, and I will hear you.
Jeremiah 29:12

And whatever you ask in prayer, you will receive, if you have faith.
Matthew 21:22

And this is the confidence that we have toward him, that if we ask anything according to his will he hears us. And if we know that he hears us in whatever we ask, we know that we have the requests that we have asked of him.
1 John 5:14-15

Confess your faults one to another, and pray one for another, that ye may be healed. The effectual fervent prayer of a righteous man availeth much.
James 5:16

WHAT THE BIBLE SAYS ABOUT:
PEACE

Now may the Lord of peace himself give you peace at all times in every way.
The Lord be with you all.
2 Thessalonians 3:16

You keep him in perfect peace whose mind is stayed on you, because he trusts in you.
Isaiah 26:3

Blessed are the peacemakers, for they shall be called sons of God.
Matthew 5:9

If possible, so far as it depends on you, live peaceably with all.
Romans 12:18

May the God of hope fill you with all joy and peace in believing, so that by the power of the Holy Spirit you may abound in hope.
Romans 15:13

Strive for peace with everyone, and for the holiness without which no one will see the Lord.
Hebrews 12:14

Deceit is in the heart of those who devise evil, but those who plan peace have joy.
Proverbs 12:20

In peace I will both lie down and sleep; for you alone, O LORD, make me dwell in safety.
Psalms 4:8

For God is not a God of confusion but of peace.
1 Corinthians 14:33

When a man's ways please the LORD, he makes even his enemies to be at peace with him.
Proverbs 16:7

And let the peace of Christ rule in your hearts, to which indeed you were called in one body. And be thankful.
Colossians 3:15

WHAT THE BIBLE SAYS ABOUT:
PERSISTENCE

Therefore, my beloved brothers, be steadfast, immovable, always abounding in the work of the Lord, knowing that in the Lord your labor is not in vain.
1 Corinthians 15:58

And let us not grow weary of doing good, for in due season we will reap, if we do not give up.
Galatians 6:9

And I tell you, ask, and it will be given to you; seek, and you will find; knock, and it will be opened to you. For everyone who asks receives, and the one who seeks finds, and to the one who knocks it will be opened.
Luke 11:9-10

For the righteous falls seven times and rises again,
but the wicked stumble in times of calamity.
Proverbs 24:16

Therefore, since we are surrounded by so great a cloud of witnesses, let us also lay aside every weight, and sin which clings so closely, and let us run with endurance the race that is set before us, looking to Jesus, the founder and perfecter of our faith, who for the joy that was set before him endured the cross, despising the shame, and is seated at the right hand of the throne of God.
Hebrews 12:1-2

I press on toward the goal for the prize of the upward call of God in Christ Jesus.
Philippians 3:14

And I am sure of this, that he who began a good work in you will bring it to completion at the day of Jesus Christ.
Philippians 1:6

Whoever is slothful will not roast his game, but the diligent man will get precious wealth.
Proverbs 12:27

And not only this, but we also exult in our tribulations, knowing that tribulation brings about perseverance; and perseverance, proven character; and proven character, hope.
Romans 5:3-4

WHAT THE BIBLE SAYS ABOUT:
RAISING CHILDREN

All your children shall be taught by the LORD, and great shall be the peace of your children.
Isaiah 54:13

Train up a child in the way he should go; even when he is old he will not depart from it. Proverbs 22:6

Fathers, do not provoke your children to anger, but bring them up in the discipline and instruction of the Lord.
Ephesians 6:4

Whoever spares the rod hates his son, but he who loves him is diligent to discipline him.
Proverbs 13:24

Discipline your son, and he will give you rest; he will give delight to your heart.
Proverbs 29:17

Behold, children are a heritage from the LORD, the fruit of the womb a reward.
Psalms 127:3

But Jesus said, "Let the little children come to me and do not hinder them, for to such belongs the kingdom of heaven."
Matthew 19:14

"For this child I prayed, and the LORD has granted me my petition that I made to him. Therefore I have lent him to the LORD. As long as he lives, he is lent to the LORD." And he worshiped the LORD there.
1 Samuel 1:27-28

One generation shall commend your works to another, and shall declare your mighty acts.
Psalms 145:4

And these words that I command you today shall be on your heart. You shall teach them diligently to your children, and shall talk of them when you sit in your house, and when you walk by the way, and when you lie down, and when you rise.
Deuteronomy 6:6-7

WHAT THE BIBLE SAYS ABOUT:
RELATIONSHIPS

Then the LORD God said, "It is not good that the man should be alone; I will make him a helper fit for him."
Genesis 2:18

Do not be unequally yoked with unbelievers. For what partnership has righteousness with lawlessness? Or what fellowship has light with darkness?
2 Corinthians 6:14

Do not be deceived: "Bad company ruins good morals."
1 Corinthians 15:33

Greater love has no one than this: to lay down one's life for one's friends.
John 15:13

Two are better than one, because they have a good reward for their toil. For if they fall, one will lift up his fellow. But woe to him who is alone when he falls and has not another to lift him up! Again, if two lie together, they keep warm, but how can one keep warm alone? And though a man might prevail against one who is alone, two will withstand him—a threefold cord is not quickly broken.
Ecclesiastes 4:9-12

Iron sharpens iron, and one man sharpens another.
Proverbs 27:17

Therefore encourage one another and build one another up, just as you are doing.
1 Thessalonians 5:11

A friend loves at all times, and a brother is born for adversity.
Proverbs 17:17

Make no friendship with a man given to anger, nor go with a wrathful man, lest you learn his ways and entangle yourself in a snare.
Proverbs 22:24-25

WHAT THE BIBLE SAYS ABOUT:
SALVATION

Because, if you confess with your mouth that Jesus is Lord and believe in your heart that God raised him from the dead, you will be saved.
Romans 10:9

Not everyone who says to me, 'Lord, Lord,' will enter the kingdom of heaven, but the one who does the will of my Father who is in heaven.
Matthew 7:21

Jesus said to him, "I am the way, and the truth, and the life. No one comes to the Father except through me."
John 14:6

This Jesus is the stone that was rejected by you, the builders, which has become the cornerstone. And there is salvation in no one else, for there is no other name under heaven given among men by which we must be saved.
Acts 4:11-12

For God so loved the world, that he gave his only Son, that whoever believes in him should not perish but have eternal life. For God did not send his Son into the world to condemn the world, but in order that the world might be saved through him. Whoever believes in him is not condemned, but whoever does not believe is condemned already, because he has not believed in the name of the only Son of God.
John 3:16-18

Whoever believes and is baptized will be saved, but whoever does not believe will be condemned.
Mark 16:16

Jesus answered, "Truly, truly, I say to you, unless one is born of water and the Spirit, he cannot enter the kingdom of God."
John 3:5

WHAT THE BIBLE SAYS ABOUT:
SEASONS

While the earth remains, seedtime and harvest, cold and heat, summer and winter, day and night, shall not cease.
Genesis 8:22

He changes times and seasons; he removes kings and sets up kings; he gives wisdom to the wise and knowledge to those who have understanding[.]
Daniel 2:21

Preach the word; be ready in season and out of season; reprove, rebuke, and exhort, with complete patience and teaching.
2 Timothy 4:2

The eyes of all look to you, and you give them their food in due season.
Psalms 145:15

To every thing there is a season, and a time to every purpose under the heaven:
Ecclesiastes 3:1

And let us not be weary in well doing: for in due season we shall reap, if we faint not.
Galatians 6:9

And he shall be like a tree planted by the rivers of water, that bringeth forth his fruit in his season; his leaf also shall not wither; and whatsoever he doeth shall prosper.
Psalmss 1:3

Now learn a parable of the fig tree; When his branch is yet tender, and putteth forth leaves, ye know that summer is nigh[.]
Matthew 24:32

He has made everything beautiful in its time. Also, he has put eternity into man's heart, yet so that he cannot find out what God has done from the beginning to the end.
Ecclesiastes 3:11

WHAT THE BIBLE SAYS ABOUT:
SPIRITUAL WARFARE

Put on the whole armor of God, that you may be able to stand against the schemes of the devil. For we wrestle not against flesh and blood, but against principalities, against powers, against the rulers of the darkness of this world, against spiritual wickedness in high places.
Ephesians 6:11-12

For though we walk in the flesh, we are not waging war according to the flesh. For the weapons of our warfare are not of the flesh but have divine power to destroy strongholds.
2 Corinthians 10:3-4

The LORD will cause your enemies who rise against you to be defeated before you. They shall come out against you one way and flee before you seven ways.
Deuteronomy 28:7

Behold, I have given you authority to tread on serpents and scorpions, and over all the power of the enemy, and nothing shall hurt you.
Luke 10:19

Truly, I say to you, whatever you bind on earth shall be bound in heaven, and whatever you loose on earth shall be loosed in heaven. Again I say to you, if two of you agree on earth about anything they ask, it will be done for them by my Father in heaven. For where two or three are gathered in my name, there am I among them.
Matthew 18:18-20

No weapon that is fashioned against you shall succeed, and you shall confute every tongue that rises against you in judgment. This is the heritage of the servants of the LORD and their vindication from me, declares the LORD.
Isaiah 54:17

When the servant of the man of God rose early in the morning and went out, behold, an army with horses and chariots was all around the city. And the servant said, "Alas, my master! What shall we do?" 16 He said, "Do not be afraid, for those who are with us are more than those who are with them."
2 Kings 6:15-16

They will make war on the Lamb, and the Lamb will conquer them, for he is Lord of lords and King of kings, and those with him are called and chosen and faithful.
Revelation 17:14

WHAT THE BIBLE SAYS ABOUT:
SUCCESS

This Book of the Law shall not depart from your mouth, but you shall meditate on it day and night, so that you may be careful to do according to all that is written in it. For then you will make your way prosperous, and then you will have good success.
Joshua 1:8

I can do all things through him who strengthens me.
Philippians 4:13

Humble yourselves before the Lord, and he will exalt you.
James 4:10

Blessed is the man who walks not in the counsel of the wicked, nor stands in the way of sinners, nor sits in the seat of scoffers; but his delight is in the law of the LORD, and on his law he meditates day and night. He is like a tree planted by streams of water that yields its fruit in its season, and its leaf does not wither. In all that he does, he prospers.
Psalms 1:1-3

Blessed is the man who trusts in the LORD, whose trust is the LORD.
Jeremiah 17:7

The LORD your God will make you abundantly prosperous in all the work of your hand, in the fruit of your womb and in the fruit of your cattle and in the fruit of your ground. For the LORD will again take delight in prospering you, as he took delight in your fathers[.]
Deuteronomy 30:9

Then Saul said to David, "Blessed be you, my son David! You will do many things and will succeed in them."
1 Samuel 26:25

What then shall we say to these things? If God is for us, who can be against us?
Romans 8:31

"Listen to me, O Judah and inhabitants of Jerusalem, put your trust in the LORD your God and you will be established. Put your trust in His prophets and succeed."
2 Chronicles 20:20

WHAT THE BIBLE SAYS ABOUT:
TEAMWORK

Two are better than one, because they have a good reward for their toil. For if they fall, one will lift up his fellow. But woe to him who is alone when he falls and has not another to lift him up! Again, if two lie together, they keep warm, but how can one keep warm alone? And though a man might prevail against one who is alone, two will withstand him—a threefold cord is not quickly broken.
Ecclesiastes 4:9-12

Iron sharpens iron, and one man sharpens another.
Proverbs 27:17

We ought therefore to show hospitality to such people so that we may work together for the truth.
3 John 1:8

For example, the body is one unit and yet has many parts. As all the parts form one body, so it is with Christ. By one Spirit we were all baptized into one body. Whether we are Jewish or Greek, slave or free, God gave all of us one Spirit to drink.
1 Corinthians 12:12-13

And it is he who gifted some to be apostles, others to be prophets, others to be evangelists, and still others to be pastors and teachers, to equip the saints, to do the work of ministry, and to build up the body of the Messiah.
Ephesians 4:11-12

The evidence of the Spirit's presence is given to each person for the common good of everyone. The Spirit gives one person the ability to speak with wisdom. The same Spirit gives another person the ability to speak with knowledge.
1 Corinthians 12:7-8

Now may the God of endurance and comfort give you unity with one another in accordance with Christ Jesus, so that together you may with one voice glorify the God and Father of our Lord Jesus Christ.
Romans 15:5-6

WHAT THE BIBLE SAYS ABOUT:
TIME MANAGEMENT

Look carefully then how you walk, not as unwise but as wise, making the best use of the time, because the days are evil. Therefore do not be foolish, but understand what the will of the Lord is.
Ephesians 5:15-17

Walk in wisdom toward outsiders, making the best use of the time.
Colossians 4:5

For which of you, desiring to build a tower, does not first sit down and count the cost, whether he has enough to complete it?
Luke 14:28

But all things should be done decently and in order.
1 Corinthians 14:40

A slack hand causes poverty, but the hand of the diligent makes rich.
Proverbs 10:4

Love not sleep, lest you come to poverty; open your eyes, and you will have plenty of bread.
Proverbs 20:13

Each one's work will become manifest, for the Day will disclose it, because it will be revealed by fire, and the fire will test what sort of work each one has done.
1 Corinthians 3:13

Six days you shall work, but on the seventh day you shall rest. In plowing time and in harvest you shall rest.
Exodus 34:21

How long will you lie there, O sluggard? When will you arise from your sleep?
Proverbs 6:9

We must work the works of him who sent me while it is day; night is coming, when no one can work.
John 9:4

WHAT THE BIBLE SAYS ABOUT:
THE HOLY SPIRIT

After they prayed, the place where they were meeting was shaken. And they were all filled with the Holy Spirit and spoke the word of God boldly.
Acts 4:31

But the Helper, the Holy Spirit, whom the Father will send in my name, he will teach you all things and bring to your remembrance all that I have said to you.
John 14:26

Likewise the Spirit helps us in our weakness. For we do not know what to pray for as we ought, but the Spirit himself intercedes for us with groanings too deep for words.
Romans 8:26

But the fruit of the Spirit is love, joy, peace, patience, kindness, goodness, faithfulness, gentleness, self-control; against such things there is no law.
Galatians 5:22-23

And Peter said to them, "Repent and be baptized every one of you in the name of Jesus Christ for the forgiveness of your sins, and you will receive the gift of the Holy Spirit.
Acts 2:38

And the Spirit of the LORD shall rest upon him, the Spirit of wisdom and understanding, the Spirit of counsel and might, the Spirit of knowledge and the fear of the LORD.
Isaiah 11:2

I still have many things to say to you, but you cannot bear them now. When the Spirit of truth comes, he will guide you into all the truth, for he will not speak on his own authority, but whatever he hears he will speak, and he will declare to you the things that are to come.
John 16:12-13

But you will receive power when the Holy Spirit has come upon you, and you will be my witnesses in Jerusalem and in all Judea and Samaria, and to the end of the earth.
Acts 1:8

Now the Lord is the Spirit, and where the Spirit of the Lord is, there is freedom.
2 Corinthians 3:17

WHAT THE BIBLE SAYS ABOUT:
THE SPOKEN WORD

Death and life are in the power of the tongue: and they that love it shall eat the fruit thereof.
Proverbs 18:21

Let no corrupting talk come out of your mouths, but only such as is good for building up, as fits the occasion, that it may give grace to those who hear.
Ephesians 4:29

Let the words of my mouth and the meditation of my heart be acceptable in your sight, O LORD, my rock and my redeemer.
Psalms 19:14

But now you must put them all away: anger, wrath, malice, slander, and obscene talk from your mouth.
Colossians 3:8

So shall my word be that goes out from my mouth; it shall not return to me empty, but it shall accomplish that which I purpose, and shall succeed in the thing for which I sent it.
Isaiah 55:11

Let your speech always be gracious, seasoned with salt, so that you may know how you ought to answer each person.
Colossians 4:6

For I will give you a mouth and wisdom, which all your adversaries shall not be able to gainsay nor resist.
Luke 21:15

The Lord GOD hath given me the tongue of the learned, that I should know how to speak a word in season to him that is weary: he wakeneth morning by morning, he wakeneth mine ear to hear as the learned.
Isaiah 50:4

It is not what goes into the mouth that defiles a person, but what comes out of the mouth; this defiles a person.
Matthew 15:11

WHAT THE BIBLE SAYS ABOUT:
TITHING/GIVING

Honor the LORD with your wealth and with the first fruits of all your produce[.]
Proverbs 3:9

Give, and it will be given to you. Good measure, pressed down, shaken together, running over, will be put into your lap. For with the measure you use it will be measured back to you.
Luke 6:38

You shall tithe all the yield of your seed that comes from the field year by year.
Deuteronomy 14:22

Will man rob God? Yet you are robbing me. But you say, 'How have we robbed you?' In your tithes and contributions. You are cursed with a curse, for you are robbing me, the whole nation of you. Bring the full tithe into the storehouse, that there may be food in my house. And thereby put me to the test, says the LORD of hosts, if I will not open the windows of heaven for you and pour down for you a blessing until there is no more need. I will rebuke the devourer for you, so that it will not destroy the fruits of your soil, and your vine in the field shall not fail to bear, says the LORD of hosts. Then all nations will call you blessed, for you will be a land of delight, says the LORD of hosts.
Malachi 3:8-12

In all things I have shown you that by working hard in this way we must help the weak and remember the words of the Lord Jesus, how he himself said, "It is more blessed to give than to receive."
Acts 20:35

There was not a needy person among them, for as many as were owners of lands or houses sold them and brought the proceeds of what was sold and laid it at the apostles' feet, and it was distributed to each as any had need.
Acts 4:34-35

Each one must give as he has decided in his heart, not reluctantly or under compulsion, for God loves a cheerful giver.
2 Corinthians 9:7

WHAT THE BIBLE SAYS ABOUT:
UNITY

Knowing their thoughts, he said to them, "Every kingdom divided against itself is laid waste, and no city or house divided against itself will stand."
Matthew 12:25

Complete my joy by being of the same mind, having the same love, being in full accord and of one mind.
Philippians 2:2

Finally, all of you, have unity of mind, sympathy, brotherly love, a tender heart, and a humble mind.
1 Peter 3:8

I appeal to you, brothers, by the name of our Lord Jesus Christ, that all of you agree, and that there be no divisions among you, but that you be united in the same mind and the same judgment.
1 Corinthians 1:10

I therefore, a prisoner for the Lord, urge you to walk in a manner worthy of the calling to which you have been called, with all humility and gentleness, with patience, bearing with one another in love, eager to maintain the unity of the Spirit in the bond of peace. There is one body and one Spirit—just as you were called to the one hope that belongs to your call— one Lord, one faith, one baptism, one God and Father of all, who is over all and through all and in all.
Ephesians 4:1-6

That together you may with one voice glorify the God and Father of our Lord Jesus Christ.
Romans 15:6

A Song of Ascents. Of David. Behold, how good and pleasant it is when brothers dwell in unity!
Psalms 133:1

As for a person who stirs up division, after warning him once and then twice, have nothing more to do with him, knowing that such a person is warped and sinful; he is self-condemned.
Titus 3:10-11

WHAT THE BIBLE SAYS ABOUT:
WISDOM

If any of you lacks wisdom, let him ask God, who gives generously to all without reproach, and it will be given him.
James 1:5

Think over what I say, for the Lord will give you understanding in everything.
2 Timothy 2:7

Trust in the LORD with all thine heart; and lean not unto thine own understanding. In all thy ways acknowledge him, and he shall direct thy paths.
Proverbs 3:5-6

For I will give you a mouth and wisdom, which none of your adversaries will be able to withstand or contradict.
Luke 21:15

Apply your heart to instruction and your ear to words of knowledge.
Proverbs 23:12

Whoever walks with the wise becomes wise, but the companion of fools will suffer harm. Proverbs 13:20

Give instruction to a wise man, and he will be still wiser; teach a righteous man, and he will increase in learning. The fear of the LORD is the beginning of wisdom, and the knowledge of the Holy One is insight.
Proverbs 9:9-10

How much better to get wisdom than gold! To get understanding is to be chosen rather than silver.
Proverbs 16:16

Let no one deceive himself. If anyone among you thinks that he is wise in this age, let him become a fool that he may become wise.
1 Corinthians 3:18

If the iron is blunt, and one does not sharpen the edge, he must use more strength, but wisdom helps one to succeed.
Ecclesiastes 10:10

WHAT THE BIBLE SAYS ABOUT:
WORK

Commit your work to the LORD, and your plans will be established.
Proverbs 16:3

Whatever you do, work heartily, as for the Lord and not for men, knowing that from the Lord you will receive the inheritance as your reward. You are serving the Lord Christ.
Colossians 3:23-24

Whoever is slack in his work is a brother to him who destroys.
Proverbs 18:9

For even when we were with you, we would give you this command: If anyone is not willing to work, let him not eat.
2 Thessalonians 3:10

Do not labor for the food that perishes, but for the food that endures to eternal life, which the Son of Man will give to you. For on him God the Father has set his seal.
John 6:27

In all toil there is profit, but mere talk tends only to poverty.
Proverbs 14:23

Let the favor of the Lord our God be upon us, and establish the work of our hands upon us; yes, establish the work of our hands!
Psalms 90:17

The hand of the diligent will rule, while the slothful will be put to forced labor.
Proverbs 12:24

The LORD shall open unto thee his good treasure, the heaven to give the rain unto thy land in his season, and to bless all the work of thine hand: and thou shalt lend unto many nations, and thou shalt not borrow.
Deuteronomy 28:12

Arise, for it is your task, and we are with you; be strong and do it.
Ezra 10:4

BLESSED AND UNSTOPPABLE

HOW TO WALK IN VICTORY

THE TEN COMMANDMENTS

The Ten Commandments can be found in the Bible, both in *Exodus 20:2-17* and *Deuteronomy 5:6-21.*

> 1. You shall have no other gods before Me.
> 2. You shall make no idols.
> 3. You shall not take the name of the Lord your God in vain.
> 4. Keep the Sabbath day holy.
> 5. Honor your father and your mother.
> 6. You shall not murder.
> 7. You shall not commit adultery.
> 8. You shall not steal.
> 9. You shall not bear false witness against your neighbor.
> 10. You shall not covet.

JESUS SUMS UP THE LAW

Jesus sums up the Ten Commandments for us in an easy and understandable way in this passage:

> *One of them, an expert in the law, tested him with this question: "Teacher, which is the greatest commandment in the Law?" Jesus replied: "'Love the Lord your God with all your heart and with all your soul and with all your mind.' This is the first and greatest commandment. And the second is like it: 'Love your neighbor as yourself.' All the Law and the Prophets hang on these two commandments."*
> *(Matthew 22:35-40)*

THE FRUITS OF THE SPIRIT

The nine attributes of a Christian life are defined in the Bible in *Galatians 5:22-23*. Every decision you make from this point forward should be <u>filtered</u> through these Biblical principles.

1. Love
2. Joy
3. Peace
4. Patience
5. Kindness
6. Goodness
7. Faithfulness
8. Gentleness
9. Self-control

SALAVATION IS AVAILABLE TO ALL

If you declare with your mouth, "Jesus is Lord," and believe in your heart that God raised him from the dead, you will be saved. For it is with your heart that you believe and are justified, and it is with your mouth that you profess your faith and are saved. As Scripture says, "Anyone who believes in him will never be put to shame."[For there is no difference between Jew and Gentile—the same Lord is Lord of all and richly blesses all who call on him, for, "Everyone who calls on the name of the Lord will be saved."
Romans 10:9-13

The 3 Steps to Getting Saved:

1. Believe in your heart that Jesus Christ died on the cross for your sins and that God raised Him from the dead.
2. Confess out loud that "Jesus is Lord."
3. Call on Him, ask Him to save you. Jesus promised, for everyone that asketh receiveth. (Matthew 7:8)

THE SINNER'S PRAYER

Pray this prayer with sincerity to receive salvation.

Heavenly Father, I confess that I am a sinner. I repent and ask for your forgiveness for all that I have done against you. I believe that your son, Jesus Christ, died on the cross for my sins and on the third day He rose again. I fully accept Him into my heart as Lord and Savior and surrender my life to you. Father, as you fill me with the Holy Spirit, I ask that you cleanse, mold, and shape me into the person you want me to be. In Jesus' name, Amen.

Congratulations!
You are now a born again Child of God. Follow up on your commitment to Christ by doing these 4 steps next.

1. Get baptized in water as commanded by Christ
2. Tell others that you accepted Christ into your heart.
3. Spend time with God every day praying and reading the Bible.
4. Seek fellowship with other believers.